YOUR BATTLES
BELONG
TO THE LORD

YOUR BATTLES BELONG TO THE LORD

Know Your Enemy and Be More
Than a Conqueror

JOYCE MEYER

FaithWords

NEW YORK NASHVILLE

FaithWords
Hachette Book Group
1290 Avenue of the Americas, New York, NY 10104
faithwords.com
twitter.com/faithwords

First Edition: September 2019

FaithWords is a division of Hachette Book Group, Inc. The FaithWords name and logo are trademarks of Hachette Book Group, Inc.

The publisher is not responsible for websites (or their content) that are not owned by the publisher.

The Hachette Speakers Bureau provides a wide range of authors for speaking events. To find out more, go to www.hachettespeakersbureau.com or call (866) 376-6591.

Library of Congress Cataloging-in-Publication Data has been applied for.

ISBNs: 978-1-5460-2627-3 (hardcover), 978-1-5460-3845-0 (large type), 978-1-5460-3727-9 (international), 978-1-5460-2625-9 (ebook)

Printed in the United States of America

LSC-H

10 9 8 7 6 5 4 3 2 1

CONTENTS

INTRODUCTION

The title of this book probably provokes excitement in most people because we feel that we are fighting something most of the time. Very few people can say they have no challenges and everything in their lives is peaceful and pleasant. There are, of course, times when we can say that everything is working out perfectly, but that is never a permanent situation.

We encounter a variety of trials, challenges, and problems, which we often call our "battles" in life. These battles may be in our relationships, our finances, or our health. They may also involve the death of a loved one or uncertainty about a decision we need to make. We live fast-paced lives and rarely have a day when everything goes as perfectly as we planned.

Jesus never promised us a life without trouble or opposition. In fact, He promised just the opposite. He said that in the world we would have tribulation, distress, and suffering. If we were to stop there, we would have to be discouraged, but Jesus also said that in Him, we could have perfect peace, that we would be courageous, confident, undaunted, and filled with joy because He has overcome the world (see John 16:33).

In this one Scripture, John 16:33, we discover what to expect in life. We can expect that if we truly believe that our battles belong to the Lord and we learn how to let God fight them for us, then any time we have trouble it will always end in victory for us. No matter how difficult our challenges are, if God is with us, we have all we need to win every battle. We should always remember that all things are possible with God (see Matt. 19:26). His strength shows itself best through our weaknesses (see 2 Cor. 12:9), and the more we lean on Him, the more we will succeed at whatever we do.

One of the people I write about in this book is Gideon. He was a frightened man who had no confidence, and God called him to fight a battle that seemed impossible to win. In the end he did win, but first, God cut the size of his army significantly so they would be massively outnumbered in the battle and have no choice but to trust Him completely. We don't win our battles because of the size of our army, because of the earthly resources at our disposal, or because of anything else that may be in our favor. We win only because our battles belong to the Lord. God gives us the victory, and to Him belong the gratitude and the praise.

When we let God fight our battles, we always win, but if we try to fight them ourselves, we always lose. However, it is important for me to establish in the beginning of this book that just because our battles belong to the Lord, it does not mean we can become passive, inactive, and lazy. It does mean that we don't take action until God shows us what to do and when to do it. Until then, we wait on Him expectantly. We take our position as His child; we stand in faith against the enemy; and we praise and worship God, fully expecting Him to instruct us, deliver us, and lead us to victory. As we learn to let God fight our battles, we can actually learn how to enjoy life while we are waiting for victory, and we can have peace in the depths of our being while storms rage on the surface of our lives through circumstances.

In this book you will learn to know your enemy. You will learn to know his nature and tactics and how to recognize and defeat him. D. Martyn Lloyd-Jones wrote in his book *The Christian Warfare*, "What a wise teacher does is to expound the Epistles, and especially this teaching concerning the wiles of the devil. All our problems arise ultimately from that source" (Carlisle, PA: Banner of Truth Trust, 1976, p. 99). I want you to know your enemy and to realize that you need not fear him. I also want you to be educated and equipped with all the information you need about his tactics, deceits, and schemes, and to learn how to recognize and defeat him.

It is obvious that two forces are at work in the world—good and evil. God is good, and the devil is evil. Since the devil cannot get to God to hurt Him, he fights against His children—those who have believed in Jesus as Savior and Lord and have been born again into His Kingdom. He hopes to hurt God through hurting us, but God has made His plan clear and it is simply this: "The Son of God appeared for this purpose, to destroy the works of the devil" (1 John 3:8).

In Romans 12:21, the apostle Paul writes that we overcome evil with good. Our natural inclination would be to return evil for evil, but that is not how we win spiritual battles against the devil and his demon hosts. He hopes to anger us and provoke us to act on that anger, but Jesus teaches us to love one another. Love is the most powerful force in the world; Satan has no way to win against true love. Luke writes in Acts 10:38 that Jesus went about doing good and healing all who were oppressed by the devil because God was with Him. He overcame evil with good, and we can, too.

I believe you will learn in this book that God not only wants to fight our battles, He wants to teach us how to fight *in a way that assures victory*. Some of this may be surprising and seem that it simply cannot work, but God's ways always work if we remain steadfast, and follow Him into battle and all the way through to victory!

Get ready to have your mind renewed and your thinking changed as you learn the truth of God's Word concerning the battles in your life. Your fight is not against people or even with circumstances, but against the devil. Paul writes:

> For our struggle is not against flesh and blood [contending only with physical opponents], but against the rulers, against the powers, against the world forces of this [present] darkness, against the spiritual forces of wickedness in the heavenly (supernatural) places.
>
> Ephesians 6:12

Your battles belong to the Lord, and the victory belongs to you! Learn to trust God to fight with you and for you, and in the midst of all your earthly struggles, you will be more than a conqueror through Jesus Christ who loves you (see Rom. 8:37).

YOUR BATTLES
BELONG
TO THE LORD

CHAPTER 1

Know Your Enemy

Be sober [well balanced and self-disciplined], be alert and cautious at all times. That enemy of yours, the devil, prowls around like a roaring lion [fiercely hungry], seeking someone to devour.

1 Peter 5:8

Satan prowls around looking for someone to devour, but that person doesn't have to be you! If you get to know him and his tactics, and if you remain watchful and alert, you can avoid being deceived and trapped by him.

This humorous story is one way to look at how powerful the devil truly is:

> Carl Armerding recounted his experience of watching a wildcat in a zoo.
>
> "As I stood there," he said, "an attendant entered the cage through a door on the opposite side. He had nothing in his hands but a broom. Carefully closing the door, he proceeded to sweep the floor of the cage." He observed that the worker had no weapon to ward off an attack by the beast. In fact, when he got to the corner of the cage where the wildcat was lying, he poked the animal with the broom. The wildcat hissed at him and then lay down

in another corner of the enclosure. Armerding remarked to the attendant, "You certainly are a brave man."

"No, I ain't brave," he replied as he continued to sweep.

"Well, then, that cat must be tame."

"No," came the reply, "he ain't tame."

"If you aren't brave and the wildcat isn't tame, then I can't understand why he doesn't attack you."

Armerding said the man chuckled, then replied with an air of confidence, "Mister, he's old—and he ain't got no teeth."

Moody Monthly, as quoted in
sermonillustrations.com

I am not implying that Satan doesn't have power. He does, and we should take that fact seriously. But let's remember that he is not actually a roaring lion, he comes *like* a roaring lion! Jesus is the Lion of the Tribe of Judah, and Satan can only portray an imitation of what is real and true. The devil is a liar, and he can only harm people who believe him and are deceived by him.

> The devil is a liar, and he can only harm people who believe him and are deceived by him.

Before we even begin to think about spiritual warfare and how to defeat the enemy, we should realize that we do not have to *try* to defeat the devil, because he is already a defeated foe. Jesus defeated him on the cross, and we merely apply by faith the victory that is already ours through our faith in Christ.

When He had disarmed the rulers and authorities [those supernatural forces of evil operating against us], He made

a public example of them [exhibiting them as captives in
His triumphal procession], having triumphed over them
through the cross.

Colossians 2:15

We know that Jesus has rescued us from darkness and trans-
ferred us into the kingdom of light, which is God's Kingdom (see
Col. 1:13).

Scripture helps us realize that we are fighting from a vantage
point of already having victory, rather than trying to win a victory. As Paul writes to the Romans, "Yet in all these things we are
more than conquerors and gain an overwhelming victory through
Him who loved us [so much that He died for us]" (Rom. 8:37).

The way we see ourselves is very important. We should see
ourselves as people with authority, as conquerors and victorious
believers. If we allow the devil to convince us that we are weak,
incapable, unable, and losers, then we will believe and demonstrate those characteristics. We should agree with God and
believe what He says about us.

One of Satan's main objectives is to prevent us from knowing who we are in Christ and knowing what our privileges are
as children of God. He works tirelessly to try to make us feel
bad about ourselves and believe we are not acceptable to God or
anyone else. As I stated above, what we believe about ourselves
is very important. It is more important than what anyone else
thinks.

Believing what God says about us in His Word and seeing ourselves as He sees us is one way we let Him fight our battles for
us. We know before the battles even begin that we have the victory. We may have to walk through some difficulties and stand

> *Satan is a defeated foe and he knows that. But if we don't know it, he will take advantage of that lack of knowledge and bluff his way into intimidating us.*

strong in faith, but we know how the story ends. Satan is a defeated foe and he knows that. But if we don't know it, he will take advantage of that lack of knowledge and bluff his way into intimidating us.

The Devil Is a Liar

The first time Satan appears in the Bible is in Genesis 3, and the first thing he does is attempt to make Eve suspicious of God's word. The devil is a liar, but God is truth and therefore He cannot lie. When Eve listened to the devil, she began to question God's goodness, and she took Satan's bait and disobeyed God's instructions to her and Adam. God said they could eat of every tree in the garden except the tree of the knowledge of good and evil. He told them not to eat of that one or they would die (see Gen. 2:17). God's instructions were for Adam and Eve's good, but the devil made them sound as though God was depriving them of something they should have and enjoy.

Like the worker in the zoo who knew the wildcat had no teeth and was too old to harm him, we can know that Satan has no real power except the power we give him through believing his lies. To believe a lie is to be deceived, but when people are deceived, they are not aware that they are deceived. They believe that what they *think* is true and they act accordingly. One of the most difficult tasks I have encountered in ministry is to try to convince someone who is deeply deceived that they are wrong about what they believe.

Not only is the devil a liar, he is the father of lies. Jesus said to a group of people listening to Him teach, "You are of your father the devil, and it is your will to practice the desires [which are characteristic] of your father. He was a murderer from the beginning, and does not stand in the truth because there is no truth in him. When he lies, he speaks what is natural to him, for he is a liar and the father of lies and half-truths" (John 8:44).

Let's think for a moment about how the fact that the devil is a liar affects our lives. If we are unaware of Satan as a real threat and if we do not know his character, he can easily deceive us and we can end up believing many things that are not true. These beliefs will keep us from enjoying the life that Jesus died for us to have.

What if you lived all your life in poverty, barely getting by, and when you were ready to die someone told you that your grandparents had left you an inheritance and you had been a millionaire for the past forty years? You could have enjoyed a totally different life than you had, but you didn't know anything about the inheritance, so you missed out on it even though it was yours all along. This is what our lives are like when we believe Satan's lies and do not know the truth of God's Word. The spiritual and material riches of Christ's inheritance are amazing, but we miss out on them because we lack knowledge of them. The truth is God wants to bless us with good things, and the devil wants to steal them from us.

Stop and ask yourself what lies you might be believing right now that are preventing you from entering into the fullness of the life Jesus wants you to have.

I can share my own experience as an example, and I am confident that many people have had similar experiences. I was a born-again Christian and attended church regularly. I even became involved in activities and various ministry outreaches at the church. I attended two different churches within a particular denomination over a period of nine years, and although I did hear the devil mentioned, I had no real concept of him as my personal enemy. I had no idea he was actively working against God, His work on the earth, and His children.

My life was like the lives of most of the Christians I knew. Although I attended church and believed in Jesus, I had no true victory. I was easily angered, negative, resentful, unforgiving, jealous, and critical. I had many other ungodly traits that were being instigated by the devil, but I did not know he was behind them or recognize him as a real enemy. Rather than seeing him as the source of my problems, I usually blamed other people and thought that if they would change, I could be happy and easier to get along with.

Blaming others for our problems is another of Satan's deceptions, and it also started in the Garden of Eden. When Adam and Eve were caught in their sin, Eve blamed the devil and Adam blamed Eve, but God assigned responsibility and punishment to all of them. Satan was guilty of lying to Adam and Eve, but they were guilty of listening and believing what he said instead of what God had said (see Gen. 3:1–19).

As long as we blame other people for our own bad behavior and problems, we are caught in a never-ending cycle of misery. The only path to freedom is letting God show us truth, facing it, and asking Him to help us change. If we have been treated unjustly, God will vindicate us in due time.

The Devil Is Alive and Active

Corrie ten Boom said, "The first step on the way to victory is to recognize the enemy." She was right!

In the 1970s I read a book that was popular at the time called *Satan Is Alive and Well on Planet Earth*, by Hal Lindsey. The book opened my eyes to many things, and God used it to start a revolutionary spiritual change in me. It introduced me to how active

Satan is on the earth and to what he is attempting to do. For the first time I saw him as a real enemy that had to be dealt with. I also became aware that many of my beliefs were just plain wrong, according to Scripture. The devil had deceived me, and I was totally unaware of it.

For example, I believed for years that because I had been abused sexually by my father, I would always have a second-rate life. I was convinced that my life could never be as good as it would have been had I not been abused. This thinking made me resentful and left me feeling hopeless. But as I learned the truth of God's Word, I discovered promises from God, such as the one that He would give me a double blessing for my former trouble and unjust treatment:

> Instead of your [former] shame you will have a double portion; and instead of humiliation your people will shout for joy over their portion. Therefore in their land they will possess double [what they had forfeited]; everlasting joy will be theirs. For I, the LORD, love justice; I hate robbery with a burnt offering. And I will faithfully reward them, and make an everlasting covenant with them.
>
> Isaiah 61:7–8

I believed I was a disappointment to God and that I should have done something to get out of my situation as a child, although I had no idea what that would have been. I told my mom what my father was doing to me, and she didn't believe me. A few years later, she even caught my father abusing me, but due to fear she decided to ignore it and not deal with it at all. I asked other relatives for help, and they didn't want to get involved. So I just gave up and decided that if I couldn't get away from the situation, I would survive it and leave home as soon as I was old enough to do so. When I did leave home, I thought I left my problem behind, but I carried it with me in my wounded soul, and sadly, suffered many more years of mental and emotional torment because I continued to believe the devil's lies.

I carried a burden of guilt and shame with me at all times, and not until I had studied God's Word for many years did the truth finally become stronger than the lies I had believed most of my life. Thankfully I learned that Jesus bore my sin, guilt, and shame, and that through my faith in Jesus, God considered me to be in right standing with Him. I was, in fact, according to Scripture, the righteousness of God in Christ (see 2 Cor. 5:21). I was a new creature in Christ; old things had passed away and all things had become brand-new (see 2 Cor. 5:17).

I learned that I had authority over Satan, and that I was called and anointed by God to serve Him and do amazing things. I also read that there are 5,467 promises from God in His Word, and I was missing out on most of them through believing Satan's lies instead of knowing the truth. Jesus said that if we know the truth, it will make us free (see John 8:32). That is what has happened to me and to millions of others, and it will happen for you also.

These examples are only a few of the lies that God's Word uncovered in my life, lies that Satan told me and I believed. I learned firsthand that the devil is indeed alive and well and active against God's people.

Taking Back Your Mind

Watchman Nee did some phenomenal writing about how Satan attacks and uses the minds of believers to do his evil work. Through his writings, I learned that the mind is the battlefield on which we either win or lose the war with evil. In his book *The Spiritual Man*, he wrote:

> Why is the Christian's mental life so beset by evil spirits?
> This can be answered in one sentence: believers afford the
> evil spirits (or the devil) the opportunity to attack.

Why would believers give evil spirits the opportunity to attack their minds? They would do so only because they are ignorant of the devil's wiles and methods of deception, or perhaps they are ignorant of his existence entirely. The word *wily*, which is related to the word *wiles*, means "cunning, crafty, and deceitful." Wiles are often described as "clever tricks," and they are Satan's way of gaining entrance into a person's life. Satan doesn't knock on the front door of our lives announcing his arrival, telling us who he is and informing us that he has come to destroy us. He lies in wait for an opportune time and then he lies, deceives, and cunningly and craftily makes his way in, often undetected. Then he delights in hearing us blame God or other people for the trouble the devil himself is instigating.

D. Martyn Lloyd-Jones observed in *The Christian Warfare*, "There is nothing, I would say, which is more significant about evangelicalism in this present century than the way in which it has largely ignored this teaching concerning the devil and the principalities and powers, and the 'wiles' of the devil" (p. 98). We need to learn a great deal in this area. Not only do we need to learn it, we also need to remind ourselves often that we have an enemy who is always on the prowl, looking for someone to devour.

People who do not learn to think for themselves are headed for trouble. Do you ever think about what you have been thinking about? If you would, then you would often find the source of your problems. Our words, emotions, and actions are the results of our thoughts. For example, it is impossible to spend the day entertaining and meditating on negative thoughts and remain happy and joyful. When our thoughts are negative and sour, our mood becomes the same. When they are positive and hopeful, our spirits lift and we live with an expectation that something good is headed our way.

> *We should choose our thoughts carefully because they ultimately become the blueprint for our lives.*

The Bible tells us to resist the devil (see James 4:7), but we often unknowingly assist him through receiving as our own any and every thought he puts into our minds. You and I can and should do our own thinking. We should choose our thoughts carefully because they ultimately become the blueprint for our lives. Paul writes in his letter to the Corinthian church:

> The weapons of our warfare are not physical [weapons of flesh and blood]. Our weapons are divinely powerful for the destruction of fortresses. We are destroying sophisticated arguments and every exalted and proud thing that sets itself up against the [true] knowledge of God, and we are taking every thought and purpose captive to the obedience of Christ.
>
> 2 Corinthians 10:4–5

People who desire to win their battles must understand the importance of this passage. First, it teaches us that we have weapons. Our weapons are not physical, so they must be spiritual. They cannot be seen in the natural realm, but they certainly affect this realm. The primary weapon Paul is talking about in

2 Corinthians 10:4–5 is the Word of God. With that Word, we recognize and defeat the lies and thoughts the devil whispers to our minds. Please notice that *we* must take those thoughts captive. It's not something God or anyone else can do for us. We direct our thoughts into obedience to the will of Christ. We learn to think as God wants us to think, and He wants us to think according to His Word. He wants us to be in agreement with Him and with His plan and purpose for our lives and His Kingdom.

Renewing Your Mind

The renewal of the mind is the most important thing for the person who has accepted Jesus as Savior and Lord. The new believer must learn to think in an entirely new way. We might have had years of practice thinking in ways that are contrary to what God says, and learning to think in agreement with God's Word will take time, education, and effort. Paul writes that we are not to be conformed to this world, but to "be transformed and progressively changed [as you mature spiritually] by the renewing of your mind [focusing on godly values and ethical attitudes]" (Rom. 12:2). In other words, we are not to think or behave as worldly people do. Instead, we are to be transformed by renewing our minds according to God's Word so we may prove what God's will is and experience the good plan and purpose He has for each one of us.

The word *transformed* as used in Romans 12:2 means "to be changed completely according to a new inner reality." God does this work in us. We become a new creation (see 2 Cor. 5:17), and as we learn to think and behave according to that new reality, our entire life changes. This happens gradually and depends on our gaining knowledge of God's Word, will, and ways, and on our willingness to submit our thinking and actions to it.

If we allow ourselves to be conformed to the world, we will think as they tell us to think and do what they tell us to do. But thankfully, as children of God, we have another option—to be transformed into the image of Christ and live the wonderful life He has provided for us through His death and resurrection.

The devil fights relentlessly against the good plan God has for us, and he does it through lies, deceptions, and various strategies, attempting to keep us distracted through sending trouble and difficulties our way. New believers are trying to grow in their relationship with Jesus through studying the Word of God because this is how they learn right from wrong. The Holy Spirit, Who lives in us and is our Helper in life, as well as our Teacher, sows the Word into our hearts, but Satan comes immediately and tries to steal it in many ways.

Jesus said that there are times when the seed (God's Word) is sown, but trouble and persecution come before it has time to take root. Immediately those who hear it are offended and displeased, and they fall away (see Mark 4:16–17). This often happens to people who have the mistaken idea that being a Christian means that God will make everything comfortable and wonderful for them. Teaching arises occasionally from different parts of the Body of Christ asserting that all the believer needs to do is look to Christ and He will give the victory. But Paul writes that we are to put on the full armor of God and to cast down thoughts that don't agree with God's Word (see Eph. 6:11; 2 Cor. 10:5).

We can see that God has given us responsibility in this process. He never fails to do His part, but He won't do our part for us. He wants us to actively participate with Him. We are partners with God in His work.

It's so important to understand this because standing firm in faith is especially challenging when we go through trials and tribulations. When the enemy is attacking believers in some way that is painful or uncomfortable for them, I frequently hear them say, "I don't understand why God let this happen. If He is good and He delivers us from our problems when we pray, then why is this happening to me?" God doesn't become angry with us when we ask such questions, but those questions are immature and typically come from immature believers, and they usually go unanswered. God wants and expects us to grow beyond making such statements when trouble comes our way. God wants to hear us say, "I trust You, Lord, and I love You just as much in hard times as I do in good ones."

I also find it interesting that we ask why negative things happen to us, but do not seem confused when other people are having trouble. We are quick to remind others that God is faithful and to encourage them to stay strong, yet when we are hurting, our thoughts and emotions can become unstable and cause us to say things we should not say.

The writer of Hebrews teaches that we should look away from all that will distract us from Jesus, who is the Author and Perfecter of our faith (see Heb. 12:2). We look to Him, and He keeps us strong and focused on the victory that is on its way. Waiting patiently in faith for breakthrough while God is fighting with us and for us is part of what we must learn to do. God promises to help us, but the timing and the way in which He does it is up to Him.

Paul makes our part clear in Ephesians 6:13:

> Therefore, put on the complete armor of God, so that you
> will be able to [successfully] resist and stand your ground
> in the evil day [of danger], and having done everything
> [that the crisis demands], to stand firm [in your place,
> fully prepared, immovable, victorious].

CHAPTER 2

Do All the Crisis Demands

...and having done everything [that the crisis demands], to stand firm [in your place, fully prepared, immovable, victorious].

Ephesians 6:13

Any time we find ourselves in any kind of crisis, it's a battle in our lives. During these times we must not remain passive or neutral. We must act! We cannot do what we do not know to do, but God expects us to do what we can. I often say that if we do what we can do while leaning on God, He will do what we cannot do as we stand in faith and wait for Him to grant us full victory. As Paul instructed, let us do all the crisis demands and then stand firmly in our place (see Eph. 6:13). As we do what we can do, we can be assured that God will fight for us and that we will always win in the end. God will fight our battles for us, but we have to show up for the fight.

It is useless to know what to do if we do not actually do it. Some people procrastinate, thinking they will do what needs to be done, but their plan is to do it later. That type of thinking is deceptive because for most of them, later is never a good time either. Procrastination is like a credit card—it is a lot of fun until you get the bill. Putting off easy things only makes them harder. Be a person of action; do what needs to be done, and never put off until tomorrow what you should do today.

I mentioned that letting God
fight our battles certainly doesn't
mean that we sit idly by and do
nothing. First, we should be very
active spiritually. We should praise

> *God will fight our battles for us, but we have to show up for the fight.*

and worship God and be thankful for all He has done for us and
for what we expect Him to do in the future. We should also lift up
our shields of faith, which quench all the fiery darts of the enemy
(see Eph. 6:16). That means we stand strong in faith, believing
God's Word and promises no matter what our circumstances may
be. We also need to continue to be faithful in prayer, not only
praying for our own needs but interceding for others as well.

During times of crisis one thing we can do is be good to other
people, helping those in trouble and meeting their needs as we
are able. I often find that although I cannot solve my own problem, God will use me to help someone else if I am willing to do so.

For example, think about a person who needs a job. Of course
that person should pray for God to give him one, but his part is
to relentlessly look for a job. A passive person might just sit by
and wait for a miracle, but a man or woman cooperating with
God and doing his or her part would not only pray but also be
aggressive in searching for employment. Such a person should be
willing to do any job he can get, even if it is not the perfect one or
the one he truly desires. Doing something fruitful while waiting
for the ideal situation is always wise. Do something or you'll do
nothing at all!

I often think of the Bible story about the sick man who lay by
the pool of Bethesda for thirty-eight years waiting for a miracle
(see John 5:1–9). He had one chance to be healed each year, when
an angel came and stirred the water. When the angel moved the
water, the first person to step into it received a miracle.

When Jesus noticed the man lying there and knew how long he had been in his infirm condition, He asked the man, "Do you want to get well?" (John 5:6). The man's response to Jesus gives us great insight into his real problem. He said he had no one to put him into the pool and that even when he tried, someone else always got ahead of him.

Both of these statements make it sound as if he was filled with self-pity. Jesus asked if the man wanted to get well, and his answer wasn't a resounding "Yes!" It was filled with excuses. Jesus didn't seem to feel sorry for the man, nor did He offer any words of sympathy, but He did tell him what to do. Jesus said, "Get up; pick up your pallet and walk" (John 5:8).

Now we might wonder what the man was supposed to do if he was so sick that all he could do was lie beside the pool for thirty-eight years. Obviously the man could walk because he told Jesus that when he tried to get in the pool, someone always beat him to it. I think it is safe to say that this man was waiting for God to fight his battles for him, but he wasn't willing to do what the crisis demanded while he was waiting.

I think the man was sicker in his soul than he was in his body. His attitude was filled with *I can't*, and when that is the case for people, just like this man, they don't even try. I don't know how far the man could walk or even how often he managed the strength to walk at all, but surely in thirty-eight years he could have wiggled his way over to the edge of the pool to assure that he would be the first to fall into the water when the angel came.

Do Something

Doing nothing is a terrible waste of the abilities that God has given us. Even if we cannot do what needs to be done in our unique situation, we can always do something. I was recently reminded of a principle that I'd forgotten: When we're faced with a project that seems insurmountable, the best way to tackle it is a little bit at a time. We can do anything if we just do what we can do no matter how tiny it might be. For example, if your closet or office needs to be cleared of excess clutter, then work ten to fifteen minutes each day on it, and soon it will be a finished project instead of one that makes you feel overwhelmed and guilty.

I once read an article about reducing stress, and it said that messy work or living spaces make us feel stressed. I know that is true for me. I feel a lot calmer and in charge of my life if my surroundings are neat and organized. But I am the only one who can keep them that way, and doing so requires constant vigilance. I must do a little something on a regular basis in order to end up with what I want.

Most of us offer excuses for our lack of effort instead of taking responsibility and simply doing what needs to be done, but that is the absolute worst choice we can make. Making excuses imprisons

> *Most of us offer excuses for our lack of effort instead of taking responsibility and simply doing what needs to be done.*

us in deception and keeps us stuck in places we dislike. I once heard that excuses are just reasons stuffed with a lie, and I think that's true.

We live in a society in which being irresponsible is becoming more normal and acceptable than taking responsibility. This is causing problems that may put an end to life as we know it if we ignore them much longer. God has given us a lot, but He expects us to be diligent and responsible to take care of it. If we don't, we'll end up losing it.

Here are a few examples of what I'm talking about. If you live in a free country, someone paid the price for your freedom at some time, but you must do your part to keep it or it will be lost. God may have helped you get a good job, but if you don't do your part to be a valued employee, the time will come when you will lose the job. Jesus paid for our salvation and it comes to us as a gift, but we must do what needs to be done in order to resist the devil and stay strong.

The way to bring about any change is to be active and do what you can do!

By now you may be thinking, *Wait a minute, Joyce. I thought this book was about letting God fight my battles, but it seems that you keep telling me what I need to do.*

Letting God fight our battles doesn't mean we do nothing while we wait for God to do everything. It's also not about trying to do what only God can do while we passively refuse to do what we *can* do. Someone said that between the big things we *cannot* do and the small things we *will not* do, the danger is that we will do nothing. If we don't plant seed, we don't get a harvest; and if we take no action, then nothing ever changes.

It is amazing to me how most people who do nothing expect other people to do for them what they should have done themselves. As much as God loves us, He will not do everything for us because that would just enable us to be lazy, inactive, and therefore, complacent and unhappy. The laziest person on the earth is the unhappiest person on the earth. Why? Because God did not fill us with abilities, gifts, talents, strength, and creativity so we could sit around and do nothing.

> The laziest person on the earth is the unhappiest person on the earth.

We either use what we have or we end up losing it. Ask God daily to show you what you can do and also to keep you from trying to do what only He can do.

For example:

- You cannot change your spouse or your child, but you can pray for God to make whatever changes He wants to make. And while you are waiting on God, you can stay busy working with the Holy Spirit to let Him make the changes in you that He wants to make.
- You cannot make people like you, but you can be a likable person.
- You cannot make your employer give you the promotion you want, but you can be the best worker he has. You can be on time, or even come in early, every day. You can go the extra mile on your job and do more than is expected of you. You can do all of this unto the Lord because of your love and appreciation for all He has done for you. Then if God chooses to promote you, it won't matter what your employer wants or thinks, because what God orders always happens.
- If you are seriously out of shape and tired all the time, and you know you need to exercise regularly, you can take small steps to become healthier. You cannot start a program and get in shape overnight, but you can begin by doing what you can do each day, even if it is only walking around the block.

When to Pray and When to Act

Once when I was praying and asking God to help someone with a problem, God whispered to my heart, "Stop asking Me to do things that you could do yourself, but just don't want to do."

What God said didn't need any interpretation. I wasn't at all confused about it, and I knew immediately that He was right. I was asking God to provide something I could easily provide, but apparently, I had not been willing to make the sacrifice necessary to do so. Inactivity is actually dangerous for the believer because when we are doing nothing, and the devil finds us passive and lazy—then he can gain access to our lives.

We should pray all the time, including times when we intend to take action. We should never take any kind of action without acknowledging God in it. For example, I might have prayed in the situation with my friend in need, "Father, _____ needs money to pay her rent this month because of an unexpected car repair. I am willing to pay it for her if that is what You would like me to do." Then, if I sense peace about my intended action, I should go ahead with it.

There are times when we pray and then act, and there are times when all we can do is pray because no action we can take will help or change our situation. We must discern between these two times and always be ready to act if we can and should do so.

Matthew 25 offers an example of people who did not do what they should have done and then expected those who had done it to get them out of trouble. In this parable, ten virgins took their lamps and went to meet the bridegroom. Five were foolish, thoughtless, silly, and careless, but the other five were diligent, wise, far-sighted, practical, and sensible.

The bridegroom was delayed and they all fell asleep, but the extra wait was no problem for the wise because they had brought extra oil with them just in case they had to wait longer than expected. The foolish ones didn't consider bringing extra oil because they were not the type to do anything extra. When the bridegroom did come, the foolish virgins were not ready and were left behind, but the wise went into the wedding feast. This story ends with this instruction:

Therefore, be on the alert [be prepared and ready], for you do not know the day nor the hour [when the Son of Man will come].

Matthew 25:13

In other words, stay active, always doing what you can do, because that is the safest course of action. Letting God fight our battles doesn't render us passive and inactive, but it does assure us that we don't need to be stressed trying to do things we cannot do or don't know how to do. God will fight for us!

Evil Isn't God's Fault

Many people say the reason they cannot or will not believe in God is because they see so much evil in the world. Their reasoning is that if God were good as people say He is, He would not allow all the hunger, murder, violence, drug addiction, homelessness, and other equally vile things we see around us or in the news each day. My question is: Are we waiting on God to solve all of these problems, or is He waiting on us? Think about this story:

A certain preacher and an atheistic barber were once walking through the city slums.

Said the barber to the preacher: "This is why I cannot believe in a God of love. If God was as kind as you say, He would not permit all this poverty, disease, and squalor. He would not allow these poor bums to be addicted to dope and other character-destroying habits. No, I cannot believe in a God who permits these things."

The minister was silent until they met a man who was especially unkempt and filthy. His hair was hanging down his neck, and he had a half-inch of stubble on his face.

Said the minister: "You can't be a very good barber or you wouldn't permit a man like that to continue living in this neighborhood without a haircut and a shave."

Indignantly the barber answered: "Why blame me for that man's condition? I can't help it that he is like that. He has never come to my shop. I could fix him up and make him look like a gentleman!"

Giving the barber a penetrating look, the minister said: "Then don't blame God for allowing people to continue in their evil ways, when He is constantly inviting them to come and be saved."

from "The Preacher and the Atheist
Barber," sermonillustrator.org

We can easily see from this story that most of the world's problems could be solved if only the people with the problems would do what they could do, or if other people who are praying for them would do what they could do. We have many problems in our world today. Actually there are so many problems that I admit they seem overwhelming, but perhaps of all of our problems the biggest one is not doing what we can do. We cannot do it all, but we must refuse to do nothing.

So any person who knows what is right to do but does not do it, to him it is sin.

James 4:17

CHAPTER 3

The Battle Belongs to the Lord

Be not afraid or dismayed at this great multitude, for the battle is not yours, but God's.

2 Chronicles 20:15

A great multitude was coming against King Jehoshaphat and all of Judah. When the king heard the report about this attack he was afraid. That is a normal response when we hear bad news, but it doesn't have to be our final response. No matter how bad the report is, if we remember that God is on our side, we can move quickly from fear to faith.

As soon as Jehoshaphat heard the report and felt afraid, he determined to seek the Lord—not only to seek Him, but to earnestly seek Him "as his vital need" (see 2 Chron. 20:3). He also proclaimed a fast throughout all of Judah. He did not waste any time starting to seek God seriously.

I love this story in 2 Chronicles because it teaches us many lessons, one of which is that when the battle is more than we can handle, God tells us we don't have to be dismayed because the battle is His, not ours.

We see clearly in this story the principle that I am writing about, which is that we should do what we can do and let God do what we cannot do. Jehoshaphat couldn't win the battle because too many groups of people had joined together to defeat him and

Judah. Seeking God was something he could do, and he wasted no time beginning to do so. He sought God diligently and seriously as his vital need. When something is considered vital, it usually means we cannot live without it. Jehoshaphat knew he was doomed to defeat unless God showed him what to do.

The people gathered together and sought help from God. According to 2 Chronicles 20:4, they were longing for Him with all their hearts. When we read this, we can sense their desperation and the depth of their realization that without God, they had no way to win the battle.

Another thing Jehoshaphat could do, and that he did, was give God praise for His power and majesty and confess that no one was able to stand against Him (see 2 Chron. 20:6). We should follow this example of seeking God and giving Him praise for all His marvelous acts. Sadly, many of us who become afraid when we get bad news begin to verbalize our fear or disappointment instead. We complain and may call our friends or our pastor to ask for advice. This is not what Jehoshaphat did, and it is not what we should do, either. Our first response to any problem should be to seek God while simultaneously giving Him praise for His greatness.

Next, Jehoshaphat reminded God that He had previously driven out these same enemies and given His people Israel the land. He actually reminded God that He gave it forever to the descendants of Abraham (see 2 Chron. 20:7). He said they had lived in the land and built God a sanctuary in it for His Name.

He also reminded God of the times they had stood before the sanctuary they had built to honor Him, confessing, "If evil comes on us, or the sword of judgment, or plague, or famine, we will stand before this house and before You (for Your Name and Your Presence is in this house) and we will cry out to You in our distress, and You will hear and save us" (2 Chronicles 20:9).

I hope you are seeing the wisdom Jehoshaphat used in approaching God. He had not yet made a petition for help with his problem, but he had sought God, fasted, given praise, and reminded God that He had given them the land. Only after doing all that did he mention his problem. But once again he reminded God that He would not allow Israel to invade those nations when they came from Egypt, and now their enemies were "rewarding" them by coming to drive them out of the land God had given to them as an inheritance (see verses 10–11).

I continue to be amazed by the wisdom of the way Jehoshaphat spoke with God and presented his problem. He respectfully told God that the problem was His: First, He gave them the land. Second, He wouldn't let them destroy these same enemies when they could have done so. And third, the land and the people in it belonged to Him anyway.

Admit Total Dependence on God

The next thing that Jehoshaphat did was very powerful, and it is something we all need to do in times of battle. He admitted total and complete dependence on God.

> "O our God, will You not judge them? For we are powerless
> against this great multitude which is coming against us.
> We do not know what to do, but our eyes are on You."
>
> 2 Chronicles 20:12

Jesus says that apart from Him we can do nothing (see John 15:5), and the sooner we learn this truth the more battles we will win. He is the Vine and we are the branches, and no branch can survive very long if it is separated from the Vine, which is its life source. I think it is wise to verbalize our dependence on God several times a day. "God, I need You. I am nothing without You, and I can do nothing without You." These are powerful confessions

> God leads and we follow!
> Nothing works if that order
> is reversed.

that please God and remind us of the position that belongs to Him in our lives, which is first place. God leads and we follow! Nothing works if that order is reversed.

After the people declare that their eyes are on God, they wait!

> So all Judah stood before the Lord, with their infants, their wives, and their children.
>
> 2 Chronicles 20:13

Scripture does not tell us how long they waited, but I sense they were prepared to wait as long as it took for God to speak to them because they knew they would be defeated without Him. How long are you prepared to wait on God in order to get clear direction from Him? I think God knows our hearts, and if we are determined not to move without His direction, we can be assured that it will come at just the right time.

As they waited the Spirit of God came upon Jahaziel and he said, "Listen carefully, all [you people of] Judah, and you inhabitants of Jerusalem, and King Jehoshaphat. The LORD says this to you: 'Be not afraid or dismayed at this great multitude, for the battle is not yours, but God's'" (2 Chronicles 20:15).

Can you imagine the relief they felt when God spoke through Jahaziel? I am sure that excitement spread through the crowd who had been waiting to hear from God. They might have wondered what exactly the message meant. Was there anything God wanted them to do, or should they just keep standing there?

Perhaps they should just go back to their homes? They had to be wondering what was next, and God told them.

He said they were to go down against the enemy tomorrow, and He told them exactly where they would find them. Then He said these crucial words:

> "You need not fight in this battle; take your positions, stand and witness the salvation of the LORD who is with you, O Judah and Jerusalem. Do not fear or be dismayed; tomorrow go out against them, for the LORD is with you."
>
> 2 Chronicles 20:17

This seems a bit odd. They were told to go out against their enemies, but they were also told they would not need to fight. In this verse God said something else of great importance, which we don't want to miss. He said, "Take your position." The people obviously knew what their position should be, because the next verse says, "Jehoshaphat bowed with his face to the ground, and all Judah...fell down before the LORD, worshiping Him. The Levites, from the sons of the Kohathites and the sons of the Korahites, stood up to praise the LORD God of Israel, with a very loud voice" (2 Chronicles 20:18–19).

Some bowed and worshipped while others stood and praised with loud voices. In this instance their battle position was one of praise and worship! They did have something to do, but it was perhaps a little different from what they would have normally done in a battle.

J. Oswald Sanders in his book *Enjoying Intimacy with God* quoted John R. W. Stott, who said, "We evangelicals do not know much about worship. Evangelism is our specialty, not worship. We have little sense of the greatness of Almighty God. We tend to be cocky, flippant, and proud. And our worship services are often ill-prepared, slovenly, mechanical, perfunctory, and dull…Much of our public worship is ritual without reality, form without power, religion without God" (Grand Rapids, MI: Discovery House, 2000, p. 23).

J. Oswald Sanders himself said, "Worship is simply the adoring contemplation of God" (Ibid.). There is a time for our petitions, but during worship we are not asking for anything. We are simply focused on God and how amazingly wonderful He is. When we have a problem, our first response is more than likely to petition (ask) God to help us with our problem. But King Jehoshaphat didn't do that.

After worshipping, Jehoshaphat reminded the people to believe and trust in God and to believe and trust in His prophets, and they would succeed (see 2 Chron. 20:20). Sometimes we simply need to be reminded to continue trusting God. Perhaps some of the people were so afraid that they struggled to believe, so the king reminded them to stay strong in faith all the way through their situation. The same is true for us when we are facing battles. We may not always understand why God is dealing with our need the way He is, but our part is to continue trusting Him.

Then King Jehoshaphat consulted with the people and "he appointed those who sang to the LORD and those who praised Him in their holy (priestly) attire, as they went out before the army and said, 'Praise and give thanks to the LORD, for His mercy and lovingkindness endure forever'" (2 Chronicles 20:21).

These instructions were very specific: They needed to be dressed in the right attire, and they were to speak specific words. Try to get a mental picture of what this must have looked like to Judah's enemies: They were ready for a fierce battle—a military conflict—and what they see is Jehoshaphat bowing with his face to the ground in worship and all the inhabitants of Judah doing the same. People were praising God with a very loud voice and singers were singing, thanking God for His mercy and lovingkindness, which endure forever.

In the remainder of the story we find that the Lord caused confusion to come upon the enemy and they actually started killing one another. They continued to do so until they were all dead. The enemy wiped themselves out. As the men of Judah went to the lookout tower, all they saw were dead bodies lying on the ground. No one escaped (see 2 Chron. 20:22–24).

Your Battlefield Becomes Your Place of Blessing

To me the end of this story is one of the best parts. Jehoshaphat and his people went to battle to take the spoils of war. This means they took what was left of their enemies' weapons, equipment, garments, goods, and other valuables. There was so much plunder to carry away that it took them three days to accomplish the job. On the fourth day they renamed the place where the battle was fought the Valley of Beracah, meaning "valley of blessings."

Their battlefield literally became their place of blessing. Many of us can make the same statement regarding battles we have fought. We have been through things that ended up making

> *Their battlefield literally became their place of blessing.*

us stronger in faith or more spiritually mature than we were prior to them. I can ask any crowd I speak to: "How many of you would say you were made better by the battles you have fought?" And without a doubt, almost all hands go up.

Are you ready for your battleground to become a valley of blessing for you? As you learn to live in the reality that your battles belong to the Lord, it will begin to happen.

Whatever else God may instruct us to do in battle, we can always be consistent in worship and praise, and we can always be thankful. Our problems never indicate that God is not good. He is good all the time and that will never change. A simple truth to remember is this: God is good, and the devil is bad!

Worship Wins Battles

Worship goes beyond petition. It does not ask God for anything; it is not occupied with the worshipper's need or problem, but it is focused on God alone. Worship is an act of paying reverence and honor to God. It is the bowing of our innermost spirit before Him in deepest humility. At the moment of worship we are fully aware that God is everything, that we are nothing, and that we can do nothing without Him. Worship leads us into a deeper level of intimacy with God.

The word *worship* means "to prostrate oneself or to bow down." I believe this can and should be done in the heart as well as with the physical body. We can worship in our hearts even if we are in a place where prostrating ourselves or bowing down would not be appropriate.

Worship can even be wordless, as Psalm 62:5 indicates: "For God alone my soul waits in silence and quietly submits to Him, for my hope is from Him." Worship can consist of one word, such as *Father. Jesus. Master.*

We have seen that worship was the deciding factor in Jehoshaphat's battle. It was also the game changer in a battle we read about in Exodus, when Israel faced Amalek and his people at Rephidim. In that story, Moses instructed Joshua to choose men to go out and fight against them and said he would stand on the top of the hill with the staff of God in his hand. As long as Moses held up his hand (indicating worship), Israel prevailed. When he lowered his hand due to fatigue, Amalek prevailed. When Moses grew tired, his men sat him on a stone and held his hands up for him.

> But Moses' hands were heavy and he grew tired. So they took a stone and put it under him, and he sat on it. Then Aaron and Hur held up his hands, one on one side and one on the other side; so it was that his hands were steady until the sun set. So Joshua overwhelmed and defeated Amalek and his people with the edge of the sword.
>
> Exodus 17:12–13

Let us remember what we have learned from the story of Jehoshaphat and the people of Judah, and the story of Moses and the Israelites fighting against Amalek, next time we are facing an enemy and need help from God:

- Seek God before anything or anyone else.
- Worship and praise Him.
- Remember other victories God has given you.
- Admit your total dependence on God.
- Stay strong in faith, keeping your eyes on God for the answer you need.
- Wait on God to speak or give you direction.
- And whatever God says to you, do it!

If God gives you something to do, do it. If He leads you to worship, be obedient to do that. The key to winning our battles, or letting God fight our battles, is not doing nothing; it's in *not* taking action of our own volition without consulting and getting direction from Him.

CHAPTER 4

Eliminate Fear

If you want to conquer fear, don't sit home and think about it. Go out and get busy.

Dale Carnegie

The fact that many of the great men and women we read about in the Bible struggled with fear did not keep God from giving them something to do. And we don't get to sit and watch the world go by just because we feel afraid. God has given us faith, and that is what we use to overcome fear. We can feel afraid and still step out and do great things by faith.

Never Take Counsel of Your Fears

During World War II, a military governor met with General George Patton in Sicily. When he praised Patton highly for his courage and bravery, the general replied, "Sir, I am not a brave man... The truth is, I am an utter, craven coward. I have never been within the sound of gunshot or in sight of battle in my whole life that I wasn't so scared that I had sweat in the palms of my hands."

Years later, when Patton's autobiography was published, it contained this significant statement by the general: "I learned very early in my life never to take counsel of my fears."

Source unknown

Fear will never stop trying to talk to us, but we don't have to take the counsel (advice) of our fears. Recognize fear for what it is—the devil trying to stop you from doing what you believe you should be doing.

> *Fear will never stop trying to talk to us, but we don't have to take the counsel (advice) of our fears.*

Esther

Esther is a young woman we read about in the Bible who was asked to do something outside of her comfort zone, something she certainly wasn't expecting. When Esther received her instructions from God through her uncle, Mordecai, she was afraid she would be put to death if she took the action she was being asked to take. Her uncle did not take pity on her and release her from her duty, but he did tell her that she had a chance to help her people and that if she didn't do it, God would find someone else. Thankfully, she pressed through her fears and did as she was asked to do, and she ended up saving her nation. (Read the Book of Esther for the full story.)

How many opportunities do we miss to do great things because we listen to our fears instead of listening to God?

Moses

Another example is found in Numbers 13, when Moses sent twelve spies into the land of Canaan to see how difficult the battle would be to take the land for the Israelites. He wanted these men to assess "whether the people who live there are strong or weak, few or many, and whether the land in which they live is good or bad, and whether the cities in which they live are [open] camps or fortifications" (Num. 13:18–19). Moses also told the spies to get some of its fruit.

When the spies returned after forty days, they reported to Moses that the land did indeed flow with milk and honey and the fruit was abundant. They also said, "But the people who live in the land are strong, and the cities are fortified (walled) and very large; moreover, we saw there the descendants of Anak [people of great stature and courage]" (Num. 13:28). Caleb told the men displaying fear to be quiet and suggested they go up at once and take possession of the land because he was sure they could conquer it. All the men, with the exception of Joshua, immediately said, "We are not able to go up against the people [of Canaan], for they are too strong for us" (Num. 13:31).

If we want to use this account to form an opinion about the percentage of people who are afraid compared to those who are not, we can easily see that the fearful far outnumber the fearless. We cannot wait to act until we don't feel any fear, or we are likely not to do anything at all. Courageous people feel the fear and move forward anyway. The question we ask should never be "Am I afraid?" but "What is God telling me to do?"

It never matters what we don't have in our favor or even how outnumbered we are. The victory depends on God, not our circumstances! Sometimes God will even put us in a position where we can't possibly win without Him—just to make sure we don't take credit for the victory. An excellent example of this is found in the story of Gideon.

Gideon

In Judges 6 we read, "The Israelites did evil in the sight of the LORD; and the LORD gave them into the hand of Midian for seven years" (v. 1). They lived in caves and mountain strongholds, and when they grew crops, the Midianites destroyed them. They took the Israelites' sheep, oxen, and donkeys, and defeated them no matter what they tried to do. Finally, because they were so impoverished and desperate, Israel cried out to the Lord.

So God sent a prophet to the Israelites to let them know that He would help them. Isn't it amazing that no matter how often Israel rebelled against God, He always came to their rescue when they cried out to Him and were ready to repent? He will do the same for us.

About the same time God sent the prophet, He also sent an angel to visit Gideon. The angel said to him, "The LORD is with you, O brave man" (Judg. 6:12). God saw Gideon as a mighty and brave man, but Gideon saw himself as weak and inadequate (see Judg. 6:11–18). It is important to note that no matter how many great things God has planned for us, unless we learn to walk by faith instead of fear, we won't do any of them.

Despite his angelic visitation, Gideon was not convinced and he said, "Please my lord, if the LORD is with us, then why has all this happened to us? And where are all His wondrous works which our fathers told us about when they said, 'Did not the LORD bring us up from Egypt?' But now the Lord has abandoned us and put us into the hand of Midian" (Judg. 6:13). Once again the Lord told Gideon to go in the strength he had and save Israel from the hand of Midian. God said, "Have I not sent you?" (Judg. 6:14).

Gideon's answers clearly show that he was blaming the Israelites' problems on God, and he was fearful rather than brave. God saw what he was capable of, but Gideon had lived in fear so long that he was totally unaware of his abilities and the fact that God was with him. He proceeded to list the reasons he was not qualified: "My family is the least [significant] in Manasseh, and I am the youngest (smallest) in my father's house" (Judg. 6:15).

The Lord answered him, "I will certainly be with you, and you will strike down the Midianites as [if they were only] one man" (Judg. 6:16). Gideon went further and asked for a sign to prove that God intended to deliver Israel through him.

> "Behold, I will put a fleece of [freshly sheared] wool on the threshing floor. If there is dew only on the fleece, and it is dry on all the ground [around it], then I will know that You will rescue Israel through me, as You have said." And it was so. When he got up early the next morning and squeezed the dew out of the fleece, he wrung from it a bowl full of water. Then Gideon said to God, "Do not let your anger burn against me, so that I may speak once more. Please let me make a test once more with the fleece; now let only the fleece be dry, and let there be dew on all the ground." God did so that night; for it was dry only on the fleece, and there was dew on all the ground [around it]."
>
> Judges 6:37–40

After these things Gideon was ready to obey God, but God told him there were too many people with him for Him to give them victory, because Israel would boast about themselves, saying, "My own power has rescued me" (see Judg. 7:2). God told Gideon to tell everyone who was afraid to go back home. Twenty-two thousand men left and ten thousand remained.

After the army decreased to ten thousand, God told Gideon there were still too many men fighting with him and prepared another test for the ten thousand who were left. Nine thousand seven hundred of the men failed that test, and that left Gideon with an army of only three hundred men. But God told Gideon that He would rescue him and turn the Midianites over to him. God did not need a huge army in order to save the Israelites from the Midianites. It doesn't matter to God if He saves by many or by few, because it is not our strength that saves us; it is our faith in Him.

Eventually the three hundred men were divided into three companies. Each had a trumpet in one hand and a pitcher with a torch inside of it in the other hand. This left them no hands with which to draw their weapons. Through a dream God gave to a man in the Midianites' camp, Gideon received instructions about how he was to defeat this army, and he relayed it to the three hundred men. They were to smash the pitchers and hold the torches in one hand and to blow their trumpets with the other hand. At the same time, they were to shout "A sword for the Lord and for Gideon!"

There is a lot more to this story, which you can read for yourself, but the bottom line is that Gideon and the Israelites enjoyed complete victory when they did what God told them to do. They put aside their own plans and let God fight their battles by simply doing as He had commanded. Even though what God told them to do perhaps made no sense to their natural minds, it worked! God's plans always work.

Anytime God seems to have put you in a position where there is no way you can win your battles, remember Gideon and go forward even if you feel afraid, knowing that the real battle belongs to the Lord.

David said to the Lord, "When I am afraid, I will put my trust and faith in You" (Ps. 56:3). I love that Scripture because David doesn't bother to try and hide his fear. He admits it and obviously believes that his fear makes no difference as long as he keeps his trust in God.

Remember that Jehoshaphat felt afraid when he learned about his enemies, but he immediately set himself to seek God. When fear knocks on your door, send faith to answer. Fear is a feeling that has only the power we give it. You can feel fear and still do anything you know you need to do, even if you "do it afraid."

> You can feel fear and still do anything you know you need to do, even if you "do it afraid."

Give God What You Don't Have

You may be scratching your head in confusion as you read the title of this section, thinking, *How can I give God what I don't have?* We should, of course, by faith give God what we do have. Our talents, abilities, finances, or strengths should be offered to God in faith for His use. But these are not the things that stop us from letting God use us. What stops us are the things we think we don't have and can't do. It is our deficits that render us fearful and inactive. These are the things we need to give to God, realizing that when we surrender our weaknesses to Him, His strength can flow through them.

When Paul was dealing with his own weaknesses, he learned this lesson, and we need to learn it also.

But He has said to me, "My grace is sufficient for you [My lovingkindness and My mercy are more than enough— always available—regardless of the situation]; for [My] power is being perfected [and is completed and shows itself most effectively] in [your] weakness."

2 Corinthians 12:9

For when I am weak [in human strength], then I am strong [truly able, truly powerful, truly drawing from God's strength].

2 Corinthians 12:10

When God called me to teach His Word, my first arguments were, "I don't know how to do that," and "I am a woman, and women don't do that." The year was 1976, and in the denomination of the church we attended at that time, women were only allowed to teach God's Word to children.

"I don't have anyone to help me" was another excuse I gave. I also said, "I don't have the proper education, and I haven't been to seminary.

"I don't have any money," I continued. I actually had quite a long list of things I thought disqualified me, but God kept assuring me in my heart that He was able to do anything I could not do, and that all I needed to do was start taking one step at a time toward what He was asking me to do. I was definitely afraid! I'm talking about the kind of fear that makes you shake and tremble. But somehow I found the courage to take one step and invite a few people to a Bible study I planned to teach. To my great surprise, they all agreed to come.

I must admit that in the natural realm, I didn't know what I was doing, but I started in the first chapter of the Gospel of John. Although I don't remember one word I said, it must have been anointed by God because people came back the following week and every week for five years after that.

Even if we don't have much in the natural, with God on our side all we need is His presence and a little bit of courage. I urge you not to let fear steal your destiny. You will never know what you can do unless you step out and find out. You will fight many battles because your enemy, the devil, will not go down quietly and easily. He will fight you every step of the way, but the Greater One (God) lives in you and He is greater than the one who comes against you (see 1 John 4:4).

This story is an example of what I am talking about.

One day, on the plains of Africa, a young buffalo named Walter approached his dad and asked him if there was anything that he should be afraid of.

"Only lions my son," his dad responded.

"Oh yes, I've heard about lions. If I ever see one, I'll turn and run as fast as I can," said Walter.

"No, that's the worst thing you can do," said the large male.

"Why? They are scary and will try to kill me."

The dad smiled and explained, "Walter, if you run away, the lions will chase you and catch you. And when they do, they will jump on your unprotected back and bring you down."

"So what should I do?" asked Walter.

"If you ever see a lion, stand your ground to show him that you're not afraid. If he doesn't move away, show him your sharp horns and stomp the ground with your hooves. If that doesn't work, move slowly towards him. If that doesn't work, charge him and hit him with everything you've got!"

"That's crazy, I'll be too scared to do that. What if he attacks me back?" said the startled young buffalo.

"Look around, Walter. What do you see?"

Walter looked around at the rest of his herd. There were about 200 massive beasts all armed with sharp horns and huge shoulders.

"If ever you're afraid, know that we are here. If you panic and run from your fears, we can't save you, but if you charge towards them, we'll be right behind you."

The young buffalo breathed deeply and nodded.

"Thanks dad, I think I understand."

We all have lions in our worlds.

There are aspects of life that scare us and make us want to run, but if we do, they will chase us down and take over our lives. Our thoughts will become dominated by the things that we are afraid of and our actions will become timid and cautious, not allowing us to reach our full potential.

James 4:7 says, "Resist the devil and he will flee from you."

So face your fears.

Show them that you're not afraid.

Show them how powerful you really are.

And run toward them with courage and boldness, knowing that we are supporting you and cheering you on.

"The Young Buffalo—A Story About Facing Your Fears," betterlifecoachingblog.com, March 22, 2013

Always remember that God and all His mighty angels are with you, and they will fight for you if you will choose to stand your ground rather than run away in fear.

Satan's Favorite Weapon

Satan uses many weapons against us in hopes of stopping us from being all that God wants us to be and having everything God wants us to have. I believe that out of them all, fear is his favorite and the one he uses most frequently.

Fear has many relatives we also need to watch out for—things like doubt, insecurity, worry, and anxiety. They present themselves in different ways, but are all connected to fear. Watch out for thoughts that come into your mind that begin with "I can't" or "I'm not."

> *Watch out for thoughts that come into your mind that begin with "I can't" or "I'm not."*

Satan stays busy trying to tell us what we are not and what we can't do, but we don't have to listen to him. If we know God's Word we can find out what we can do through Him and who we are in Him.

Satan is always negative and energy draining, but God is positive and His thoughts fill us with the courage and energy to do what needs to be done. Satan will tell us what we cannot do and then condemn us when we try something and fail. God will tell us to try, and if we fail we can try and try again. We never fail unless we stop trying and give up.

CHAPTER 5

Fully Assured

*O God, we praise Thee for keeping us till this day, and for
the full assurance that Thou wilt never let us go.*

Charles Spurgeon

The Bible teaches us that we are to approach God in full assurance of faith (see Heb. 10:22), but Satan works tirelessly to steal our assurance and cause us to doubt and feel uncertain about not only our salvation, but about many other things too.

We are told to beware of the "wiles" of the devil (see 2 Cor. 2:11 AMPC), and this lack of assurance is one of them. It is one way he cunningly and craftily attacks us and distracts us from our purpose and calling, as well as preventing us from fully enjoying our relationship with God.

Abraham, while waiting many long years for the promise of God to become a reality in his life, was fully assured that God had the power to do what He had promised (see Rom. 4:21). God had promised Abraham that he and Sarah would have a biological child, but they were both long past child-bearing age. Abraham had nothing in the natural realm to base his assurance on, but he did have a strong faith in God, and because of that he did not despair. Ultimately he did receive the full manifestation of his faith—exactly what he was believing God for! We should always remember that with God, all things are possible (see Matt. 19:26).

Complete and full assurance allows us to enter the rest of God, which means we can be at peace and fully enjoy our lives while we wait on God to do what we are trusting Him to do. However, the devil wants us to be anxious, worried, and fearful. Just think for a few moments about how wonderful your life could be if you had full assurance that God hears and answers your prayers, that you are saved and no one can snatch you from God's hand, that you are loved unconditionally, and that God will never allow more to come on you than what you can endure (see 1 Cor. 10:13). We need *full assurance*, not some assurance mixed with some doubt! Putting thoughts of doubt into our minds is one way Satan deceives us.

When we doubt or feel we have lost our assurance, we rarely think the devil has instigated it. Instead, we believe we are weak in faith and often chastise ourselves for not trusting God more. This is not to say that we have no responsibility in these matters, because it is our responsibility to recognize and resist the devil. Part of my purpose in writing this book is to help people know and recognize the lies of the devil and how he attempts to work in our lives. This will give us the information we need to resist him.

> When doubt comes, do you habitually resist the devil by reminding him that he is a liar?

When doubt comes, do you habitually resist the devil by reminding him that he is a liar? Do you reaffirm your faith in God by keeping a firm focus on God's promises in His Word and speaking them over your life? Or do you passively receive the thoughts of doubt and merely wish you were stronger in faith? Wishing is useless because it has nothing to base its desires on, whereas faith can rest on the promises of God.

We do have a responsibility to resist doubt, unbelief, loss of assurance, and all the other lies of Satan. If we are determined to do so, then the Holy Spirit will work with us and help us recognize the attacks of the devil and deal with them successfully. Christians are not meant to remain in doubt or to be uncertain. We are not meant to be passive and expect good things from God to fill our lives while we do nothing. We are meant to fight the good fight of faith (see 1 Tim. 6:12), submit ourselves to God, and resist the devil, and he will flee (see James 4:7).

Satan's First Attack

One of the first areas Satan attacks is a person's assurance of salvation. After my father repented of his sins at the age of eighty years old and asked Jesus into his heart and life, it was very difficult for him to believe he had truly been forgiven. He had indeed lived a reprehensible and especially wicked life, and in the process he hurt many people. We had to keep assuring him that he was forgiven, not because he deserved it, but because Jesus had paid for his sins.

Quite often when attending a church that invites people to come to the altar at the end of the service and receive Christ, we see some of the same people come over and over again, and this is because they have no assurance of salvation. They focus on how bad they have been instead of how good God is. God's promise to us is this: "Where sin increased, [God's remarkable, gracious gift of] grace [His unmerited favor] has surpassed it and increased all the more" (Rom. 5:20). People often have the mistaken idea that each time they sin or backslide from God, even if only for one day, then they need to be saved all over again, but this is absolutely not true.

I recall receiving Christ when I was nine years old at a church with some relatives we were visiting. At that church service I asked Jesus into my heart. I experienced the cleansing power of God and truly felt that all my sins had been forgiven. But the next day, less than twenty-four hours after my salvation, I was playing hide-and-seek with my cousins, and I was tempted to cheat and peek to see where they hid so I could find them. I succumbed to the temptation, and the thought came to me that I had lost my salvation. I continued to believe that until I was a young adult. I had no idea at the age of nine that the devil was my enemy, a liar, and it was he who put the thought in my head that robbed me of the gift God had given me.

The devil always seeks to cause confusion, and he often does that by taking people from one extreme to another. They may pray a prayer of repentance and feel exhilarated, but those feelings will eventually go away. When the feelings are gone, if they make a mistake, such as losing their temper or telling a lie, it can cause them to believe they have lost their salvation. Or the devil may even suggest that they were never really saved at all. He often reminds us of our sins and tells us that if we were truly saved, we would no longer behave in a sinful manner.

Not one of us has arrived at perfection. We are growing and becoming more spiritually mature, but we will make mistakes along the way. When we sin it doesn't mean that we are not saved; it simply means we still need to keep growing.

Jesus told His disciples that they were all clean because of the Word He had spoken to them (see John 15:3). How could that be? After all, Judas betrayed Him, Peter denied he knew Him, and they all disappointed Him when they fell asleep while He was suffering in the Garden of Gethsemane and needed them most.

In my search for an answer to this, I read one writer who said spiritual immaturity is quite different from rebellion. I agree with him wholeheartedly, and I believe this is a truth we need to fully understand. Rebellion means a person's heart is still full of wickedness and sin, but spiritual immaturity can be, and is, overcome little by little as the Christian learns the will of God and submits to it.

Judas did show remorse for betraying Jesus for thirty pieces of silver, but there is no evidence that he actually repented. Sadly, he killed himself. He fell prey to Satan's suggestions and made a huge mistake. I once read some history about Judas that said he was insecure and jealous, and we can see how that would be true. He wanted a higher position among the disciples than he had, and his attitude probably opened the door for Satan to convince him to betray Jesus for some money. In contrast Peter was repentant after his denial of Christ, so he was forgiven and God went on to use him in a very powerful way. A similar situation happened with the apostle Paul, and the mercy and grace God extended to him is amazing. He spent years zealously persecuting Christians, but he actually believed he was doing the right thing. He was full of religious zeal and later said that God gave him grace because he had zeal without knowledge.

Peter, Paul, and the other disciples continued to grow spiritually while God was using them. We mature spiritually little by little. While that process is taking place we do improve in many ways, but we continue to have weaknesses to deal with. Let me simply say that you can still enjoy yourself while you are growing spiritually. God knew every mistake you would ever make before you made it, and He loves you anyway. Don't

> *You can still enjoy yourself while you are growing spiritually.*

let Satan convince you that you have lost your salvation when you display immature behavior. Be quick to repent and ask the Holy Spirit to help you grow spiritually.

God's Word promises "that He who has begun a good work in you will [continue to] perfect and complete it until the day of Christ Jesus [the time of His return]" (Phil. 1:6). Paul said that although he had not arrived at the place of perfection he pursued so fervently, one thing was of prime importance to him—to let go of his mistakes and press on to better things (see Phil. 3:13–14). He knew that if he allowed his mistakes to fill him with guilt and condemnation, then he would stop growing beyond them and never go on to new levels of spiritual maturity. The same is true for each of us.

Walking in Forgiveness

We must learn to walk in continual forgiveness of our sins. Daily repentance should be part of our prayers. King David asked God to forgive him for sins he was unaware of (see Ps. 19:12), and I often do that myself. I learned long ago that it was unfruitful for me to live with a "sin consciousness," always being aware of every tiny mistake I made. When I realize that I have sinned, I quickly repent. Then, believing I have been forgiven according to God's promise in His Word, I forget it and go on to better things.

Some Christians have asked me what would happen to them if they should die before they have had an opportunity to repent of a sin they committed. They have been concerned they would go to hell, but that is absolutely not true. Jesus has paid for all the sins we have committed or ever will commit, and He knows our heart toward Him. He knows whether or not the person in question would have repented, and therefore He counts it as done. I urge you to break the habit of living daily life with a consciousness of all your sins and mistakes. Repent and receive forgiveness, then let go of them and press on to the things that are ahead.

Learn to live with a "righteousness consciousness" instead of a "sin consciousness." This means that we keep our thoughts focused on the fact that we are righteous before God because of what Jesus has done, and we do not dwell on what we have done wrong. To put it very simply, it means paying more attention to our righteousness than to our sin. We are made right with God through our faith in Jesus' sacrifice. No other sacrifice needs to be made for our sin. We don't have to offer God our guilt as a sacrifice for our misdeeds. We simply repent and receive complete forgiveness and walk in the assurance of that wonderful gift. We can choose to focus on being right with God, rather than thinking He is angry with us for every mistake we make and dwelling on that.

> Therefore, since we have been justified [that is, acquitted of sin, declared blameless before God] by faith, [let us grasp the fact that] we have peace with God [and the joy of reconciliation with Him] through our Lord Jesus Christ (the Messiah, the Anointed).
>
> Romans 5:1

Say to yourself daily, "I have repented of my sin and I am made right with God. He loves me unconditionally and all of my sins are forgiven." Now, walk in that knowledge of being forgiven.

Not only should we walk in God's forgiveness toward us, we should extend that same forgiveness to those who have offended or hurt us.

> Bearing graciously with one another, and willingly forgiving each other if one has a cause for complaint against another; just as the Lord has forgiven you, so should you forgive.
>
> Colossians 3:13

Ask yourself daily if you are angry with anyone, and if the Holy Spirit makes you aware that you are, then decide right then and there to forgive completely. Ask for God's help in doing so, and trust Him to bring justice in your life. Pray for your enemies, that God will bless them, because this is one of the single most powerful things you can do. If Jesus can forgive us for our many sins, then we should be able to forgive anyone else, no matter what they have done to hurt us.

> *Pray for your enemies, that God will bless them, because this is one of the single most powerful things you can do.*

The Prodigal Son

One of the Bible's greatest examples concerning God's willingness to totally forgive our sins is in the parable Jesus told about a son who wanted his inheritance early so he could leave home to do as he pleased. In his culture this action was equivalent to telling his father that he wished he were dead. In those times a son *never* discussed or asked for his inheritance.

The father gave the son his inheritance, and the young man left home and wasted his fortune in living a sinful and undisciplined life. He was eventually forced to work for a pig farmer and even eat the same food the pigs ate. The young man eventually came to his senses and decided to go home to his father. He wasn't expecting the privileges of a son, but he was ready and willing to work as a servant in his father's house. However, when his father saw him coming a long way off, he ordered his servants to bring out the most festive and best robe, to find a ring for the boy's finger and sandals for his feet, and to kill the fattened calf and prepare the finest meat for a special celebration. They were to prepare for a celebration because his son had been lost and now he was found (see Luke 15:11–32).

The amazing part of the story is that the father had already decided to forgive before the young man even repented. Perhaps the father knew his son wouldn't be coming home unless he intended to do so, but this idea is still very thought provoking. It shows the father's heart toward his children. Instead of planning the son's punishment, he planned a party!

God wants us to come to the party too. The New Testament especially is filled with instructions to have joy and to enjoy. Joy is to be the hallmark sign of Christians. We are to rejoice in our salvation and in the wonderful plan that God has for us. We do have trials and tribulations, but as Paul said, we should not allow the difficulty of these momentary afflictions to distract us from the joy that is ours in Christ.

> For our momentary, light distress [this passing trouble] is producing for us an eternal weight of glory [a fullness] beyond all measure [surpassing all comparisons, a transcendent splendor and an endless blessedness]! So we look not at the things which are seen, but at the things which are unseen; for the things which are visible are temporal [just brief and fleeting], but the things which are invisible are everlasting and imperishable.
>
> 2 Corinthians 4:17–18

One of the best and most enjoyable ways to defeat the devil in all his attacks is to remain joyful. He hates our joy because he has none of his own, and for that reason he robustly tries to steal ours.

CHAPTER 6

Assurance Concerning Prayer

To be a Christian without prayer is no more possible than to be alive without breathing.

attributed to Martin Luther

A story in *The Kneeling Christian*, written by a man using the pseudonym "Unknown Christian" and originally published in 1924, reports: "A traveler in China visited a heathen temple on a great feast day. Many were the worshipers of the hideous idol enclosed in a sacred shrine. The visitor noticed that most of the devotees brought with them small pieces of paper on which prayers had been written or printed. These they would wrap up in little mud balls and fling them at the idol. The visitor inquired the reason for this strange proceeding, and was told that if the mud ball stuck fast to the idol, then the prayer would assuredly be answered; but if the mud fell off then the prayer was rejected by God" (Peabody, MA: Hendrickson Publishers, 2006, p. xi).

We may think this is a very odd custom, but some Christians pray in similar ways. They basically fling prayers at God and wait to see if they stick or not, but they don't pray with assurance that God hears and answers.

Christians are meant to know joy and peace, and that isn't possible unless we know how to pray and have full assurance of the power of prayer. God actually needs our prayers because there is a great deal He desires to do and cannot do unless someone asks Him to do it. It seems impossible that God would need us for anything, but since He works through us, He does need us. Obviously God can do anything He chooses to without anyone's help, but He has committed Himself to partnership with His children, and that is amazing.

If we want to do much for God, then we must ask much of God. Paul says that God is able to do superabundantly more than all we dare ask or think (see Eph. 3:20). The devil desires

> *If we want to do much for God, then we must ask much of God.*

that we not pray at all, or if we do pray, that we ask for very little. He hates bold, aggressive, confident prayers. Just think of your own prayers and how often they are attacked in some way.

For example, the phone rings while you are praying and you feel compelled to answer it. Or someone has an emergency just as you are about to pray, and you have to change your plans. Or you suddenly become sleepy shortly after you begin praying, or you have difficulty focusing. Even if we succeed at putting time into prayer, the devil will immediately suggest to us that our prayers were not "right," that we didn't pray about the right things or that we didn't pray the right way. He also makes us think our prayers weren't long enough or eloquent enough. It took me a long time to realize how the devil stole from me through this method of making me feel that even if I did pray, I didn't do it right.

I have noticed frequently that after I have prayed about something, my next thought is, *That isn't going to accomplish anything. It wasn't long enough, or fervent enough.* Some Bible translations of James 5:16 tell us that the "fervent" prayer of the righteous person is powerful. The word *fervent* may give us the idea that our prayers need to be intense, and although that is one part of the definition of the word, *fervent* also means "to be sincere and heartfelt." My prayers are usually simple, but they are sincere. I think the devil wants us to believe that prayer should always be hard work and that we need to feel deep emotion concerning what we pray about. That may be the case at times, but it is the sincerity of our prayers and the faith offered with them that makes them effective, not what we feel, or whether we cry or not, or how loud or long we pray. Be cautious not to let the devil deceive you concerning the validity of your prayers. When you pray in faith, God hears and He answers in His way and in His timing.

There are times when we labor in prayer concerning a serious situation. Jesus prayed so intensely in the Garden of Gethsemane in preparation for His crucifixion that "His sweat became like drops of blood, falling down on the ground" (Luke 22:44). Epaphras wrestled in prayer for the Colossians (see Col. 4:12). While there may be labor and wrestling in prayer at times, I believe a great deal of our prayer is interwoven throughout the day and should become as simple as breathing. I like to use the phrase "Pray your way through the day."

God has taught me that if prayer is sincere, it doesn't need to be eloquent or even necessarily long. God sees our hearts, and He doesn't judge the quality of our prayers as we might think He would. He only looks at the sincerity, faith, and confidence with which we pray.

God's will is for us to be able to pray with confidence and assurance. Our prayers are not meant to be uncertain. We are not meant to be vague and doubtingly groping after God, thinking that if we're lucky, we might get an answer to our request. No! This is not true prayer. This kind of prayer doesn't receive answers from God. We are not slinging mud balls with prayer requests written on pieces of paper at God, hoping they will stick.

This is the [remarkable degree of] confidence which we
[as believers are entitled to] have before Him: that if we
ask anything according to His will, [that is, consistent
with His plan and purpose] He hears us. And if we know
[for a fact, as indeed we do] that He hears and listens to
us in whatever we ask, we [also] know [with settled and
absolute knowledge] that we have [granted to us] the
requests which we have asked from Him.

1 John 5:14–15

I recommend that you take some time and slowly read these
two verses a few times, and give much thought to the immen-
sity of what they are saying. The apostle John had full assurance
regarding answered prayer, and he desired the same assurance
for those to whom he wrote, and that includes us.

You may ask, "What if we don't pray according to God's plan
and purpose?" This Scripture indicates He only hears prayers
prayed according to His will. While it is true that God won't give
us something that is not best for us, we should rejoice in that fact
and trust that He will guide us to something even better.

One way we can be assured of praying God's will is to pray the
Scriptures. Simply take a verse or a passage of Scripture and turn
it into prayer for someone else or for yourself. This can easily
be done with 1 John 5:14–15. The prayer would sound something
like this:

"Father, I ask for a remarkable degree of confidence as I
pray. I want to pray for Your plan and purpose and I ask
that You guide me. If I do pray amiss, then I trust You will
not give me what I ask for, but that You will guide me to
ask for Your will. I believe that if I ask anything according

to Your plan, then You will hear me, and I believe with absolute assurance that You will grant the request I make of You. Thank You, Father. I ask it in Jesus' name!"

You may follow this same pattern with almost any Scripture.

There are, of course, many things you will want and need to pray about that are not specifically covered by Bible verses. We should always pray that these be granted to us only if it is God's will. We can pray with assurance that God will give us His will and that it will come at the exact right time in the exact right way!

The Power of Prayer

The promises of God concerning prayer are almost too incredible for us to believe, but they are true. It is good to keep a book on prayer close by and refer to it frequently as a way of keeping your faith fresh and strong. *The Kneeling Christian*, which I mentioned at the beginning of this chapter, is one I refer to frequently merely to feed my faith.

We feed our faith with God's Word, and it is wise to always feed your spirit in areas that are especially important. The power and necessity of prayer is at the top of the list. There are countless great books on prayer, so find one that is helpful to you and simple to read, and use it often. One that might help and encourage you is my book *The Power of Simple Prayer*.

The Unknown Christian writes in his book that when we get to heaven and see things from God's viewpoint, we will be astonished that we didn't pray more and wonder why we let this power slip by us untapped so many times. It could only be because we are still learning how important and powerful prayer is. I think we can learn to live in an attitude of prayer, always having our hearts uplifted to God while knowing we need His help in all we do.

The apostle James mentions Elijah and says that although he was a man with appetites and passions like ours, he prayed and God did amazing things. Elijah wasn't a perfect man, just as we are not perfect, but that didn't stop him from praying, and it must not stop us (see James 5:17). Satan will tell us we are not good enough to pray and that we especially are not good enough to expect God to do much for us. But remember that Satan is a liar and that he hates prayer. He works diligently to persuade us to neglect prayer. I think it is safe to say that Satan is afraid of our prayers. He knows that when we pray, God moves on our behalf to do

> *I think it is safe to say that Satan is afraid of our prayers.*

things that will ultimately prevent him from accomplishing the evil he has planned for us. We should remember how powerful prayer is, and that Satan will do anything and everything he can to keep us from praying with confidence.

The Four "Wows" of Prayer

There are four promises in John 14, 15, and 16 that I call the four "wows" of prayer. We often use the word *wow* to describe something so amazing we simply don't know what else to say. The scriptural promises regarding prayer that I want to share with you in this section are definitely wow material.

Before we go over the Scriptures, I would like to ask you to think about and make a decision to believe the promises they present. We may read many things that could be helpful to us, but if we don't believe them strongly enough to act on the information, then it is useless to us. Since effective prayer is such an important part of spiritual warfare, we will do well to believe everything God's Word says about it.

- **Wow # 1**: "Truly, truly, I say to you, whoever believes in me will also do the works that I do; and greater works than these will he do, because I am going to the Father. Whatever you ask in my name, this I will do, that the Father may be glorified in the Son. If you ask me anything in my name, I will do it" (John 14:12–14 ESV).
- **Wow #2**: "If you abide in Me, and My words abide in you, you will ask what you desire, and it shall be done for you. By this My Father is glorified, that you bear much fruit; so you will be My disciples" (John 15:7–8 NKJV).
- **Wow #3**: "You did not choose Me but I chose you, and appointed you that you would go and bear fruit, and that your fruit would remain, so that whatever you ask of the Father in My name He may give to you" (John 15:16 NASB).
- **Wow #4**: "Until now you have asked nothing in my name. Ask, and you will receive, that your joy may be full" (John 16:24 ESV).

These four Scriptures make incredible promises, and we should believe them and pray not out of obligation or as a religious duty, but in anticipation and joy. If we believe these promises, what could possibly keep us from praying?

Prayer not only helps us in our times of need, but it helps and strengthens us always, enabling us to bear much fruit for God's Kingdom.

Hindrances to Answered Prayer

Satan knows we can accomplish more through our prayers than we can through our work, and he does his utmost to hinder our prayers. He would rather we do anything other than pray.

There are many hindrances to having our prayers answered, but I would like to mention just four of them.

1. Hidden Sin

The first hindrance to answered prayer is hidden sin. God's Word says that if we hide iniquity in our hearts, God will not hear us (see Ps. 66:18). I recommend that we begin our prayers by repenting of all sin known or unknown because we want to approach God with clean, pure hearts.

2. Doubt

Doubt is a second hindrance to answered prayer. For this reason Satan tries to steal our assurance concerning prayer. He doesn't want us to pray, but if we do, he wants us to doubt the validity of our prayers or to wonder if they will be answered. James tells us that we can ask God for help when we need it and that He will give it without reproach or faultfinding—but the request must be in faith, with no doubting or wavering (see James 1:5–8).

In case the phrase "without reproach or faultfinding" is unfamiliar to you, let me explain it in my own words. If you have made mistakes and gotten yourself into a mess, and you realize you need God's help, go ahead and ask for it. He will help you, and He won't make you feel guilty or ashamed of what you have done in the process. God won't say, "I'll help you, but you sure don't deserve it after what you did." He wants us to have a repentant heart and come boldly and ask for the help we need.

I cannot say I never have any doubt, so when I do I am honest with God. I try to follow the example of the father who went to Jesus to ask for his child's healing. Jesus asked the father if he believed, and he told Jesus that he did believe, but needed help with his unbelief (see Mark 9:20–24).

The father's doubt did not prevent him from receiving the help he sought. If we focus on the great faith we do have rather than the little bit of doubt we may have, I believe we will also see answers to our prayers.

3. Selfishness

Selfishness is a third hindrance to answered prayer. Selfishness is all about me and what I want, with no concern for others. God's Word teaches us to live exactly the opposite from this. We are to forget ourselves, entrust ourselves to God, and live to help, please, and make others happy.

> We are to forget ourselves, entrust ourselves to God, and live to help, please, and make others happy.

I think it is safe to say that overcoming selfishness is a lifetime challenge. I never have to try to be selfish, but oftentimes I do have to remind myself to not be selfish. Even in prayer I think our natural inclination is to pray for what we want and need first and foremost. But remember the prayer of Jehoshaphat, and recall that his request was at the bottom of his list while praise and gratitude were at the top.

God gives all of us the ministry of intercession, which means we have the privilege of praying for others. The Holy Spirit may lead you to pray for someone who does not know how to pray, or you may be led to join your prayers with those of someone who is already praying but needs some added strength. The more we unify in prayer, the more powerful our prayers become. I know when I am sick or going through something difficult, I want as many people praying for me as possible, and I am sure you do also. There is certainly nothing wrong with asking God for what we want and need, but if that is all we do when we pray, it is selfish and may hinder our prayers from being answered.

4. Refusing to Forgive

Without a doubt, the refusal to forgive those who have hurt us is the biggest hindrance to answered prayer. God has stated plainly that if we don't forgive others their offenses against us, He cannot forgive us ours (see Matt. 6:15).

The Bible teaches us that we can ask God for anything and if we believe we have received it, we will get it. Please notice that we don't always get it immediately, but if we will believe in our heart that God has heard our prayer and that we have received what we have asked for, then when the right time comes, we will get it (see Mark 11:23–24). This is a great promise, but we must read it in the context of the next verse, which says:

> "Whenever you stand praying, if you have anything against anyone, forgive him [drop the issue, let it go], so that your Father who is in heaven will also forgive you your transgressions and wrongdoings [against Him and others]."
>
> Mark 11:25

I remember reading a statement from Watchman Nee, saying that most of the ground Satan gains in the lives of believers is due to the fact that they are not willing to forgive those who have hurt them or treated them unfairly.

Prayer is far too important for us to allow these obstacles or anything else to hinder its effectiveness. Oh God, let us be assured of the power of prayer and help us pray often.

CHAPTER 7

Ways the Devil Tries to Deceive People

And the great dragon was thrown down, that ancient ser-pent, who is called the devil and Satan, the deceiver of the whole world.

Revelation 12:9 ESV

Satan devours people through deception. When we are deceived, we believe lies we have been told, but since we do not know they are lies, we accept them as truth and act according to them. It is imperative that children of God know the difference between the lies of Satan and the truth of God's Word; otherwise they can be kept in bondage all of their lives. They will also miss out on the privileges and wonderful lives God has planned for them.

Here are a few examples of how deception operates:

- You may believe you are incapable of doing something that God has actually enabled you to do.
- You may believe you can never completely get over a painful past.
- You may believe you have no value, or that God doesn't love you because no matter how hard you try, you always seem to mess up and make mistakes.

None of these things are true, but if you believe them, then Satan has deceived you and his lies have become your reality.

One of our first defenses against deception is prayer. Jesus said we should pray and be careful not to be deceived (see Matt. 24:4). He also said that in the last days deception would increase (see Matt. 24:24). Right now, the general consensus is that we are living in the last days. Society today continually sends us the message that there is no absolute truth; truth is ever changing and based on our perceptions. In other words, the truth can be one thing to one person and something else to another. Of course, that is nonsense because if truth exists at all, it is a constant standard that is the same all the time for all people.

Relativism, Humanism, and Absolute Truth

Relativism declares there are no absolutes because all things are relative to other things. The relativist states that truth is relative to a person's situation or to what he feels. People who don't believe in God or in traditional Christianity often do not believe God's Word is absolute truth. When people hold this view, it is very easy for the devil to deceive them because they have nothing concrete by which to judge anything. If you don't stand for something, you will fall for anything, and that is a dangerous position to be in.

> If you don't stand for something, you will fall for anything, and that is a dangerous position to be in.

I recently read this in an article I came across online:

> While absolute truth is a logical necessity, there are some religious orientations (atheistic humanists, for example) who argue against the existence of absolute truth. Humanism's

exclusion of God necessitates moral relativism. Humanist John Dewey (1859–1952), co-author and signer of the Humanist Manifesto 1 (1933), declared, "There is no God and there is no soul. Hence, there are no needs for the props of traditional religion. With dogma and creed excluded, then immutable truth is also dead and buried. There is no room for fixed, natural law or moral absolutes." Humanists believe one should do, as one feels is right.

from "Absolute Truth," All About…,
allaboutphilosophy.org

It seems to me that what humanists believe is no more than a good excuse to do anything they want to do with no accountability for their actions. This is the atmosphere in which anarchy can exist and eventually destroy a civilization. The anarchist refuses to recognize authority of any kind and rebellion reigns.

I don't deny relativism as a principle that must be applied in some situations, but I do say that it cannot be applied to God's Word. For example, if someone invites me to a party, whether I go or not may be relative to what kind of party it is, my schedule, or any number of other factors. But, if someone asks me if I believe God is good, then the answer is yes. That is not and never will be relative to anything else. The truth is simply that God is good. I frequently hear people say, "If God is good, then why do bad things happen to good people?" There are many answers to that question that I cannot explain in this book, but I can say that no matter what the reasons are, our problems never change the truth that God is good!

> *Our problems never change the truth that God is good!*

Absolute truth can be defined as an inflexible reality, fixed, invariable, and unalterable. We can see that the definition of *truth* is the polar opposite of relativism.

Personally, I believe God's Word is absolute truth. My understanding of His Word may grow and change as I study and am taught, but His Word is always the same. It is the standard on which I base all of my decisions and by which I measure my thoughts. It is the only way I know to recognize the lies of the devil and to prevent myself from being deceived.

Another way the devil deceives people is by presenting Jesus as a historical figure instead of as the Savior of mankind. They don't say He didn't exist, or that He wasn't powerful, but they deny that He is the Son of God. Most false religions are a mixture of some truth with some error, and that is what makes them dangerous.

To arbitrarily believe everything you read without checking into its source is not wise. Demons can easily lead people to write books filled with philosophical ideas that appeal to the human mind even though they are not true. Ideas and principles may sound reasonable, but they can ultimately lead to misery and life without God. Always remember that anyone can write a book and say anything they want to, but that doesn't make it true!

John urges believers to test and try the spirits for many false prophets are in the world (see 1 John 4:1). Luke writes in Acts about the Berean believers who received the teaching of salvation enthusiastically, but also examined the Scriptures daily to see if what they were hearing was true (see Acts 17:10–11). Test what you hear, read, and believe. Ask if it agrees with God's Word and if it truly works in your life and produces good fruit. Find the truth, hold it firmly in your heart, and never let it go.

Pray That You Won't Be Deceived

I pray regularly that God will protect me from deception, and I urge you to do the same. The world is filled with deception these days.

The influence of people who are deceived can lead us into deception and error if we do not know the truth of God's Word. We need something solid and unchanging to hold on to and keep us grounded. For me it is God's Word, and I pray it is the same for you. I have seen how the Word has influenced and changed not only my life, but also the lives of countless other people. I am completely and utterly convinced that Jesus is the Way, the Truth, and the Life (see John 14:6). You will have to decide for yourself if you believe this. If you have not already done so, I urge you to do so without delay. God is always the same and He is the rock we can stand on, the rock that never moves. Everything around us might be shifting and changing, but God is always the same, yesterday, today, and forever (see Heb. 13:8).

I read that the suicide rate in the world today is the highest it has ever been, and I believe that is due in large part to the confusion and hopelessness that people feel when they do not have a proper understanding of God and His Word. I have heard that suicide is the second-highest cause of death for adolescents twelve to nineteen years of age (cdc.gov). Why would someone who is just beginning their life feel the need to end it, if not because they see nothing to live for? People need something solid to cling to, and they need the truth rather than the philosophies of ungodly people. Most people feel they are fighting something most of the time, but many don't realize their real war is against Satan. He alone is the underlying cause, the instigator and perpetrator of what ails our society, and the only weapon that will defeat him is the truth of God's Word.

The apostle James wrote that we are to be subject to God and resist the devil, and then he will flee from us (see James 4:7). Obeying God and resisting the devil are both our responsibilities as believers. When we do this, God will fight our battles for us. We need to be diligent to know who our real enemy is, recognize the tactics he uses, and live carefully and watchfully because he is always searching for ways to influence our lives.

The apostle Paul instructs us to put on God's whole armor so we may successfully stand up to all the strategies and deceits of the devil (see Eph. 6:11). Here again is something we are responsible to do. Ephesians 6:10–18 gives us a good description of what this armor is, and we will cover it in detail in a later chapter. Satan is a dangerous foe, but God has not left us unequipped to deal with him. In fact, we have all we need to be more than conquerors.

Practical Ways to Avoid Deception

In addition to praying that we will not be deceived, there are several practical things we can do to keep deception far from us.

Manage emotions and feelings.

Nothing is more dangerous to Satan than a believer who is willing to obey God and believe His Word no matter how they feel.

> Nothing is more dangerous to Satan than a believer who is willing to obey God and believe His Word no matter how they feel.

More than anything else, people tell us how they feel, but feelings don't always tell us the truth. They are fickle! We may feel like doing one thing at 8:00 A.M., and somehow by 2:00 P.M. we no longer feel like doing it, even though we said we would do it earlier. As victorious Christians, we must learn how to manage our emotions and how to judge what we feel by God's Word to determine whether our feelings are conveying truth or deception.

Feelings can be quite motivating, but when they disappear that doesn't mean that we are free to stop doing what we have committed to do.

> Feelings can be quite motivating, but when they disappear that doesn't mean that we are free to stop doing what we have committed to do.

Avoid extremes.

1 Peter 5:8 tells us to be well-balanced, self-disciplined, alert, and cautious at all times in order to keep Satan from gaining an advantage over us. Satan doesn't care if we do too much or too little of something. As long as we are extreme he is satisfied. Consider these examples:

1. Some people may not be prudent in saving money for the future, while others may be stingy and save more than is necessary. They may hoard all they have out of fear of not having enough. In doing so they are not trusting God at all to take care of them.
2. Some people are not willing to do anything for anyone else. They are totally self-absorbed and think only of themselves. Others do too much for people, enabling them to remain lazy and inactive. Or they do so much for others that they don't take proper care of themselves, and they end up filled with resentment and feeling as if people take advantage of them.
3. Some people have no discipline at all. Others are very legalistic, living strictly by rules and regulations. This can

make them very rigid, difficult to get along with, and often critical of people who don't live as they do.

The list of extremes could go on and on, but the point is for us to work with the Holy Spirit and allow Him to lead us so we can maintain balance in all areas of life. There is a godly rhythm for our lives, and when we follow it, life is enjoyable and we avoid giving the devil an opening to torment or deceive us. We all need work and rest, fun and laughter, worship and solitude (times of quiet). We need to be alone, but we also need the balance of being in community with other people. Solomon wrote that there is a perfect time for everything (see Eccles. 3), and we have often heard that we should do all things in moderation.

Don't put your trust in works of the flesh.

One major way the devil deceives us is by provoking us to stay busy doing what the Bible calls "works of the flesh." Works of the flesh refer to our efforts to try to make something happen without leaning on God for help. God doesn't do everything for us, but neither can we do anything without Him.

The apostle Paul writes at length in his Epistles about works of the flesh and how useless and devoid of power they are. These activities keep us busy and frustrated, because they are not effective and leave us disappointed. We are saved by God's grace through faith in Jesus, and not by any works we have done. The way we are saved is the way we must learn to live our daily lives.

> We are saved by God's grace through faith in Jesus, and not by any works we have done. The way we are saved is the way we must learn to live our daily lives.

Worry is a work of our flesh that attempts to solve our own problems. As we learn to stop thinking about our problems and fill our minds instead with the truth that our battles belong to the Lord, we will be able to let God fight our battles for us and realize that worry is something we no longer have to do. As a matter of fact, God's Word teaches that when we cast our care, God takes care of us (see 1 Pet. 5:7). The more we lean and rely on God, the more He helps us.

Trying to change the people in our lives into what we want them to be is also a work of the flesh. Only God can change people. We can and should pray for them, but we cannot change them. True and lasting change must come from the inside out, and only God can change a person's heart. We should love people as they are rather than how we want them to be. God loves us unconditionally, and He wants us to love others the same way.

Learning to recognize when we are doing "works of the flesh" is very important. We waste a great deal of time and energy on what I call "works that don't work." Anytime I start trying to make something happen on my own, or trying to force something that God doesn't approve of, I become frustrated, disappointed, and worn-out. I have learned that works of the flesh produce struggle, whereas faith in God produces rest!

Refuse to compromise.

To compromise means to go a little bit below what you know to be right, and it is a major way Satan deceives people. The devil says that "just once" won't hurt. That is what he told Jesus when he tempted Him in the wilderness (see Luke 4). He said if Jesus would bow down and worship him just once, he would give Him all the kingdoms of this world (see Luke 4:5–8).

I once heard a funny story about a father whose children were trying to convince him to let them go to a movie that had a little foul language and a few inappropriate sex scenes. They argued that just a little bit wouldn't hurt them. He told them no, and then proceeded to give them an example of how dangerous just "a little bit" can be. He baked his children's favorite cookies and then told them he had added just a tiny bit of a new ingredient—dog poop—but he guaranteed them that they would not taste it at all. Not one of them was willing to try the new cookies, and Dad had made his point.

Don't believe the "just once" or "a little won't hurt" lies! Set standards, live by them, and don't compromise when others urge you to do so. Just because someone else does something, that doesn't make it right for you. Jesus said that we are in the world but we are not to be like it (see John 17:14–16; Rom. 12:2). Charles Spurgeon said, "I believe that one reason why the church of God at this present moment has so little influence over the world is because the world has so much influence over the church" (https://www.christianquotes .info/quotes-by-topic/quotes-about-compromise/#ixzz5DycJhvpl).

Paul wrote to Timothy that a soldier in service does not get entangled in the enterprises of civilian life; his aim is to satisfy the one who enlisted him (see 2 Tim. 2:4).

Satan tempts us to live two lives or to be a dual person, meaning we present ourselves as one type of person when we are with our Christian friends and as another when we are with our worldly associates. A person may behave one way at church and quite another way at the office or at home. But if our faith in Jesus is genuine and sincere, then we will be the same in every situation. We must not let the fear of what people think of us lead us to compromise our moral behavior.

Satan has scored a victory when he is successful in presenting compromising Christians to the world.

Deny deceitful desires.

Another way the devil deceives us is through the things we desire. God will give us the desires of our heart as we delight ourselves in Him (see Ps. 37:4), but He won't give us the desires of our flesh. People may desire and pursue things that have no ability to do for them what they thought they would. When they obtain these things, they may be excited for a short time, but they soon feel empty. We all seek to be happy, but sadly we may waste many years pursuing things that are what Jeremiah called empty wells with no water in them.

> "For My people have committed two evils: They have abandoned (rejected) Me, the fountain of living water, and they have carved out their own cisterns, broken cisterns that cannot hold water."
>
> Jeremiah 2:13

This kind of deception works in a way similar to how a mirage affects a person stranded in the desert. He is so thirsty that he imagines he sees a pond of water ahead. He runs for it and dives into what he thinks will quench his thirst, but sadly, finds just more sand.

God wants us to have many enjoyable things, but He must be first place in our lives. God can give us joy without things, but things without God will never give us joy.

> *God can give us joy without things, but things without God will never give us joy.*

Millions of people waste their lives chasing things they think will give them satisfaction, contentment, and joy, and they end up frustrated and discontented. It may be money, position, or higher levels of education. They may desire to be in a certain social group, or to climb a mountain, or be number one at some sport. Often people want to own things like bigger houses, better cars, boats, more expensive clothes, and all kinds of material goods.

If our goal is to obtain the things of the world, Satan can always dangle more "things" in front of us and we can waste more time chasing them. But will they really make us happy and give us peace? Apparently they won't, because some of the wealthiest and most famous people in the world are reported to be among some of the unhappiest. In fact, I was reading an article just yesterday about famous, wealthy people who spent their lives entertaining others, yet in their private lives, they suffered with terrible unhappiness, to the point that some committed suicide, believing they couldn't face another day.

Like most people, I tried all the wrong ways to find happiness until I finally exhausted all possibilities. Then, thankfully, I learned that my own desires were deceiving me. Satan was continually whispering to me, "This is it; this will make you happy once you get it." He is a liar. What we truly need to find true happiness is God and His will for our lives.

Jesus said He came that we might "enjoy life and have it in abundance" (see John 10:10). He wants us to have an abundance of all good things, but we must remember that things without God cannot give us happiness.

The ways Satan tries to deceive people are probably endless, so let's be dedicated to praying on a regular basis for God to reveal any deception in our lives, and let us live by the truth of God's Word.

CHAPTER 8

Hold Your Peace

"The LORD will fight for you, and you shall hold your peace."
Exodus 14:14 NKJV

God will fight our battles for us, but we see in Exodus 14:14 that we have a responsibility, which is to hold on to our peace. The Amplified Bible version of this verse says we are to "keep silent and remain calm." Is this challenging? Yes! Is it possible? Yes! God never tells us to do something that is not possible for us to do. It is important to believe that, otherwise the devil will fill our minds with endless excuses and reasons we cannot do what God tells us to do.

When we cut away everything that distracts us, I think what most of us want more than anything else is peace, and according to Jesus, we have it. He said that He left His peace with us—not the kind of peace the world offers, but a special peace that functions in the midst of life's storms. He also said, "Do not let your heart be troubled, nor let it be afraid" (John 14:27). We can continually see the same theme throughout the Word of God. He promises to fight for us, and that promise always comes with something He expects us to do. We could say that our action of obedience represents sowing a seed of faith, and then God brings the harvest.

The seed we sow may require some type of physical action, but not always. Sometimes the seed is a spiritual action. We believe, and God works. We pray, and God changes circumstances. We remain peaceful, and God fights our battles.

> The God of peace will soon crush Satan under your feet.
>
> Romans 16:20 ESV

Jesus is the Prince of Peace (see Isa. 9:6). He came to Earth to bring us peace and to tear down the walls that divide us. He desires that we dwell together in unity because when we do, our power increases. Peace produces power, but chaos and turmoil produce weakness. It is only natural then that Satan works tirelessly to keep people angry, worried, anxious, upset, or frustrated, and to do anything else that will steal our peace. He is the prince of chaos!

Jesus said those who are "makers and maintainers of peace" will express God's character and be called His sons (see Matt. 5:9). All believers are children of God, but not all reach the mature level of sons and daughters. Holding on to peace in the midst of tribulation is done by the spiritually mature—those who have had their senses trained by experience to trust God at all times, knowing that He always works things out for our good. I believe the more experience we have with God, the easier it becomes to trust Him. If we refuse to give up, each situation we go through shows us God's faithfulness, and over time we realize that He truly never lets us down. Things may not always turn out as we hope they will, but eventually we see that God's way is best.

Talk to Yourself

One thing that helps me calm down when I have lost my peace is to talk to myself. I have a meeting with myself and say things like this: "Joyce, worry is not going to make this better. Being upset is not good for your health. It will leave you worn out and probably grouchy." I remind myself that God is good and faithful, and that as long as I believe, He will work on my behalf. Sometimes there is nothing better than having a good talk with yourself. We can talk ourselves into being upset, or we can talk ourselves into being calm—it is up to us.

> *We can talk ourselves into being upset, or we can talk ourselves into being calm— it is up to us.*

You may remember that Exodus 14:14 says to "keep silent and remain calm," and God will fight for you. This is because we sometimes talk too much to the wrong people, or out of our frustration and fear, which causes us to say things that do not agree with God's Word. The best thing to do during a battle is to meditate on Scriptures that will help you calm down. Anytime I start to worry, I meditate on Philippians 4:6–7, which says, "Do not be anxious about anything, but in everything by prayer and supplication with thanksgiving let your requests be made known to God. And the peace of God, which surpasses all understanding, will guard your hearts and minds in Christ Jesus" (ESV).

Anyone who can worry can meditate. To worry is to meditate on a problem, to think about it over and over and over. Meditation on God's Word works the same way; we take a Scripture and think about it over and over and over. This acts like medicine for the soul and has a calming effect.

Ronald Reagan said, "Peace is not the absence of conflict, but the ability to cope with conflict by peaceful means." I have often said, "When we disagree, we can learn to disagree agreeably."

Worried people usually have scowls on their faces and furrows in their brows. It isn't difficult to spot a worried person. Mother

Teresa said, "Peace begins with a smile." I think that is a great thought. Maybe if we start by purposely smiling, our emotions will follow, bringing peace and joy.

Peace is a conscious choice, not something we merely wait to feel. God's Word instructs us to "pursue peace" (see Heb. 12:14). In Colossians 3:15, Paul teaches us to let the peace of God rule in our hearts. In other words, the presence or absence of peace should be the deciding factor in all our decisions. We need to find what is peaceful before taking any action. We would save ourselves a great deal of trouble in life if we would learn to always follow peace. I may want a new home or automobile, but if I don't have peace about the purchase, then I shouldn't do it. I may want to talk to a friend about a fault I see in her, but if I don't have peace about it, then I shouldn't say anything about it.

Just because we want to do something, or we feel like doing it or think it is a good idea, it may still be the wrong thing to do. We should slow down a little and take time to ask ourselves, "Do I have peace about the action I am about to take?" We must go deeper than our mind, will, and emotions and listen to Jesus, Who lives in our hearts and seeks to guide us through His Spirit at all times. Since He is the Prince of Peace, His approval of our intended action will always manifest in peace.

I love what Eleanor Roosevelt said: "It isn't enough to talk about peace. One must believe in it. And it isn't enough to believe in it. One must work at it."

No statement could be any truer than this one. Peace won't fall on us like rain falling on our heads. We must choose it, hang on to it, and stand fast against the devil while he continually tries to bring chaos into our lives.

The Author of Chaos

Since Jesus is the Prince of Peace, it is easy to conclude that all the turmoil and chaos, strife, war, and anger we see in the world are not from Him. Their author is Satan! He hates unity and peace, and he does all he can to infest the world with strife, hatred, unforgiveness, bitterness, resentment, offense, and war. Anything that divides people is something the devil loves and toward which he works relentlessly.

Just think about how difficult it is for even two people to dwell in peace. Then multiply that by millions, and you can easily imagine how full of chaos our world is. Divorce is rampant, and in 2017, the United States ranked twelfth in the world (platinumparalegals.com). Among churchgoers, 38 percent have been divorced, so going to church doesn't make us immune to the devil's tactics (thegospelcoalition.org). As stated earlier, we must *choose* peace. Dave and I have been married for fifty-two years, and I can tell you that there were times when we had to choose to work things out instead of walking out.

When people divorce it is because they can't get along peacefully. Although I agree that there are times when divorce is the only or perhaps even the best solution, it should be a rare occasion, not a commonplace event.

Take a Stand

If we choose to live in peace, we can't have a casual attitude toward worry and anxiety. We must take a firm stand against it and pray that God will help us defeat and overcome it in our lives. Worry shows that our faith in God is not as strong as it should be, and it steals peace from multitudes of people. There are probably more people on the earth who worry than there are those who don't. Worry is a destructive habit, and it can keep us from being productive at our jobs and from being fully present at home with our families.

Anxious thoughts plague our minds and cloud our reason, keeping us from seeing clearly. The more we fixate on a problem, the bigger it becomes. We may start worrying over a small matter, and before long we see it as a giant that torments us. People who struggle with ongoing worry and anxiety often experience sleepless nights, tossing and turning over the what-ifs running through their minds. Most of the things we worry about and fear never happen, and even if they did, their effect on us would not be as tormenting as all the worry we have endured.

Worry is a thief that robs us of peace and joy. The Bible says clearly that the devil is the thief who comes for one purpose only, which is to kill, steal, and destroy (see John 10:10). However, the good news is that Jesus came for the purpose of destroying the works of the wicked one (see 1 John 3:8). Satan was defeated when God raised Jesus from the dead and gave Him all authority in heaven and on the earth (see Matt. 28:18). Everything is under His feet, and because Jesus is "head over all things in the church," we can overcome the enemy too (see Eph. 1:22). Jesus has given us the authority that God gave Him, and we need to learn to use it. God is for us, and that means we don't have to worry.

> Jesus has given us the authority that God gave Him, and we need to learn to use it.

Jesus gave us a clear mandate not to worry, stating that worrying cannot add one single hour to our life (see Matt. 6:27). In fact, worry diminishes our quality of life. One thing that helps me when I start worrying about something is to remind myself that it won't do any good. Worry keeps me busy but accomplishes nothing. Sometimes I have to remind myself several times, but that is part of resisting the devil. He doesn't give up easily, and we must not, either.

Worry rules over us unless and until we trust that God will fight our battles for us as we continue to worship and thank Him. Believing that He is good and trusting Him with the unknown is the quickest way to find peace. We simply cannot worry and trust at the same time. Worry is hard work. One day of worry is much harder than a day of work. I encourage you to put the energy you use worrying into prayer, and I promise that you will see much better results.

> Worry does not empty tomorrow of its sorrow. It empties today of its strength.
>
> Corrie ten Boom

Two Scriptures in particular have helped me greatly as I have endeavored to live at peace:

> "He must search for peace [with God, with self, with others] and pursue it eagerly [actively—not merely desiring it]."
>
> 1 Peter 3:11

> Turn away from evil and do good; seek peace and pursue it.
>
> Psalm 34:14

Before I understood these two verses, I merely wished I had peace, and I prayed for peace. I passively waited for peace to come, thinking that if my circumstances would change, then

I could have peace. No amount of waiting passively and being inactive will ever bring us peace. We must refuse to live without it and go after it with a determination that will ultimately defeat Satan.

Peace with God, with Self, and with Others

To me a large part of the answer concerning how we can have peace lies in 1 Peter 3:11. We pursue peace with God, with self, and with others, and I think it must occur in that exact order.

Peace with God is found in repentance and receiving forgiveness for sins. We find it through developing an intimate relationship with God and realizing that He cares deeply about every area of our lives and wants to be involved in everything we do. We discover it as we come to know how much God loves us and how precious we are to Him. Receiving God's forgiveness and love allows us to learn how to forgive and love ourselves and how to be at peace with ourselves. Not one of us deserves God's help, but we can receive it by faith as a gift from Him because He is good!

Learn how to be a friend and ally to yourself. God is for you and wants to help you, but if you are against yourself, you keep a door open for the devil to torment you. God will fight for us, but we cannot be against ourselves and receive much help from Him.

We all do many things that are wrong, and the devil is quick to remind us of them. But we also do many things that are right. Learn to recognize your gifts and the things you do well, and appreciate the abilities God has given you. Focusing on the negative aspects of our lives never helps us, but it does steal our peace. We should, of course, repent of our sin and of the wrong things we do, but once we have done so, we should receive God's forgiveness and refuse to accept guilt and condemnation from the devil.

Once we have learned to love God and love ourselves, we can begin loving other people, and this is God's ultimate goal. He wants us to spread His love everywhere we go.

Enjoying peace in relationships requires learning to be quick to forgive, difficult to offend, generous in mercy, and willing to bear with people's failings and weaknesses (see Rom. 15:1). Treating others the way we want to be treated is indeed the "golden rule" (see Matt. 7:12), as it has been called. Living with that goal in mind will help us immensely to be at peace with people.

Accepting all people "as is" is the first step toward having peace with them. God does not ask us to love people as we would like them to be, but as they are. He accepts us that way, and over time His love changes us. The same principle applies to our relationships with people. Love comes first, and then comes change!

Peace of Mind

All loss of peace and upset begin in the mind. If we don't learn to guard our thoughts and understand the power they have, Satan will rule us by placing wrong and destructive thoughts in our mind continually. Learning to think about things that will benefit us should be

> *All loss of peace and upset begin in the mind.*

our constant goal. We can choose our own thoughts, and we should do so carefully. Through Christ, we have the ability to cast down wrong thoughts and imaginations. Admittedly it requires effort, but we will never enjoy peace if it doesn't begin in our thoughts.

When trouble comes we can think about all the terrible things that could happen, or we can choose to think that God is faithful and that He will fight our battles for us while we continue trusting Him and being a blessing to others. When we fail we can imagine that God is angry with us, or we can believe what God's Word teaches us about His love, forgiveness, and mercy. Likewise, when people upset or disappoint us we can meditate on their offense, but the longer we do so the angrier we will become. Or we can choose to think about the value of the person and the good things we enjoy about them. We can also choose to believe the best rather than the worst. For example, some people are not even aware they've hurt us. They may be going through something painful themselves, and what they said or did was birthed out of their own pain. Maybe they need encouragement instead of isolation.

After over forty years of teaching God's Word I am still continually amazed by the power our thoughts have over us. I often say, "Where the mind goes, the man follows." If we think upsetting thoughts, we will be upset, but if we think on good things, we will enjoy a life of peace even as we deal with problems. Paul writes that in the midst of all of our troubles we may look like sheep being led to the slaughter, but we are more than conquerors through Christ Who loves us (see Rom. 8:36–37).

As frustrating as people can be, we need them and have to find a way to dwell together in unity, or we will give the devil a foothold in our lives. As Paul teaches, we should never let the sun go down on our anger.

> Be angry [at sin—at immorality, at injustice, at ungodly
> behavior], yet do not sin; do not let your anger [cause you
> shame, nor allow it to] last until the sun goes down. And
> do not give the devil an opportunity [to lead you into sin

by holding a grudge, or nurturing anger, or harboring resentment, or cultivating bitterness].

Ephesians 4:26–27

Decide right now that you will never go to bed angry again, and you will be well on your way to enjoying a peaceful life. Don't forget: The Lord will fight for you, and you shall hold your peace (see Exod. 14:14).

CHAPTER 9

What Is the Real Problem?

For our struggle is not against flesh and blood [contending only with physical opponents], but against the rulers, against the powers, against the world forces of this [present] darkness, against the spiritual forces of wickedness in the heavenly (supernatural) places.

Ephesians 6:12

If we never learn what our real problem is, we will spend our lives fighting with things and people without solving anything. The devil loves it when we don't know or remember that he is the source of all misery, hatred, strife, turmoil, and the battles we fight. If we don't know that the devil exists and that he is our enemy, we live in great deception. He is against everything godly and good, and he is especially against God and His children (you and me).

There are, of course, real issues that must be dealt with, unpleasant circumstances and people who hurt and abuse us. But the source of all problems is Satan. In addition to bringing practical solutions to our problems, we need to resist and take authority over the devil because God has given us the responsibility and the right to do so.

We see this truth in Scripture when we read about the way

Jesus dealt with Peter when he was trying to convince Him not to go to Jerusalem to suffer.

Beginning in Matthew 16:21, Jesus "began to show His disciples [clearly] that He must go to Jerusalem, and endure many things at the hands of the elders and the chief priests and scribes (Sanhedrin, Jewish High Court), and be killed, and be raised [from death to life] on the third day." Peter's response to Jesus' announcement was improper, and Jesus rebuked him. But take a look at exactly what Jesus said to him.

> Peter took Him aside [to speak to Him privately] and began to reprimand Him, saying, "May God forbid it! This will never happen to You." But Jesus turned and said to Peter, "Get behind Me, Satan! You are a stumbling block to Me; for you are not setting your mind on things of God, but on things of man."
>
> Matthew 16:22–23

Jesus was not saying that Peter was Satan, but rather that Satan was working through Peter and attempting to divert Him from God's purpose. Satan works through various means. He works through people, even good and well-meaning people, and he creates and works through circumstances of all kinds. Satan is behind all sin, all war, all strife, all disobedience, and everything that is not in agreement with God and His Word.

Another example we see in the Bible is in the story of a couple named Ananias and Sapphira, who sold a piece of property and said they would give the proceeds from the sale to the church. However, they kept back part of the funds for themselves, and this is what Peter said to them.

But Peter said, "Ananias, why has Satan filled your heart to lie to the Holy Spirit and [secretly] keep back for yourself some of the proceeds [from the sale] of the land? As long as it remained [unsold], did it not remain your own [to do with as you pleased]? And after it was sold, was the money not under your control? Why is it that you have conceived this act [of hypocrisy and deceit] in your heart? You have not [simply] lied to people, but to God."

Acts 5:3–4

Satan was the one behind what Ananias and Sapphira did. He suggested to them that they keep part of what they had committed to give. The sin was theirs, but Satan instigated it. They evidently did not recognize his lie, nor did they consider the consequences of their actions. The same thing happens more often than we would care to admit, and it will continue happening until we recognize the true source of our problems and deal with it accordingly.

Another example we find in the Bible is when Judas betrayed Jesus.

Then Satan entered Judas, the one called Iscariot, who was one of the twelve [disciples]. And he went away and discussed with the chief priests and officers how he might betray Him and hand Him over to them. They were delighted and agreed with him to give him money.

Luke 22:3–5

The Devil Made Me Do It!

Seeing that Satan is the source of all evil doesn't mean we can brush aside our responsibility to recognize and resist him. We cannot just say, "The devil made me do it," and be passive about taking action against him.

> We cannot just say, "The devil made me do it," and be passive about taking action against him.

Since angels "do His commandments, obeying the voice of His word" (Ps. 103:20), one sure way to get their help is to say things that allow them to fight for you. "Satan, I resist you in Jesus' name" is one thing we can say to let the devil know that we recognize he is at work, that we will resist him, and that we intend to trust God to help us in our fight.

Jesus spoke to Satan, who was working through Peter, and we can use His example as a pattern for us to follow. Always use the name of Jesus when rebuking Satan, for it is that name only that has the power to defeat him.

> Always use the name of Jesus when rebuking Satan, for it is that name only that has the power to defeat him.

For this reason also [because He obeyed and so completely humbled Himself], God has highly exalted Him and bestowed on Him the name which is above every name, so that at the name of Jesus every knee shall bow [in submission], of those who are in heaven and on earth and under the earth.

Philippians 2:9–10

The name of Jesus is above every other name and carries tremendous power. Because of Jesus' extreme obedience, God filled

His name with great power. Not only did God give Jesus that powerful name, but Jesus has now given it to us to use in His place and represent Him. We have been given "power of attorney" to use the name of Jesus as if He were with us physically. I recently gave my son a power of attorney, which is a legal document allowing him to use my name in certain business matters that I would not be home to handle, so I understand how this works.

When Jesus ascended into heaven, He gave us His authority and power and His name to use in the same way He used it. Any-

> The name of Jesus is one of the most powerful gifts we have been given, and with it, we can hold back the forces of darkness.

time we use the name of Jesus it represents all that He is. The name of Jesus is one of the most powerful gifts we have been given, and with it, we can hold back the forces of darkness. All prayer is to be offered in Jesus' name.

"And I will do whatever you ask in My name [as My representative], this I will do, so that the Father may be glorified and celebrated in the Son. If you ask Me anything in My name [as My representative], I will do it."

John 14:13–14

The name of Jesus is the only name by which people can be saved (see Acts 4:11–12). We baptize them in the name of God the Father, Jesus the Son, and the Holy Spirit.

A woman once told me a story that shows the power that is in Jesus' name. She was driving with her small child in the car with her in the passenger seat. She approached an intersection and realized that a car was headed straight for the passenger side of her car. She knew that without divine intervention, there was no way to avoid an accident. She only had time to say, "Jesus." The oncoming car managed to stop just before it would have hit her car. As she spoke with the trembling man who had been driving the other vehicle and thanked him, he said, "You don't understand. I never even had time to put my foot on the brakes. Whatever stopped the car, it wasn't me!"

The battles we fight in life are not against flesh and blood. They are against Satan and his host of demonic forces, and it is our responsibility to recognize that and resist him. Authority is useless if it is not enforced, and we can reinforce the authority Jesus has given us by reminding the devil that we know he is already a defeated foe—a liar—and that although he has power, it is minor compared to the power of God that is on our side.

Jesus declares that we have been given power and authority and that nothing can ultimately harm us:

> He said to them, "I watched Satan fall from heaven like [a flash of] lightning. Listen carefully: I have given you authority [that you now possess] to tread on serpents and scorpions, and [the ability to exercise authority] over all the power of the enemy (Satan); and nothing will [in any way] harm you."
>
> Luke 10:18–19

First, I want to point out that Jesus saw Satan fall from heaven when he was cast out due to his pride and rebellion. Second, I want to point out that Satan has power, but it is no match for the power of God. Luke 10:18–19 contains no mention of Satan having authority, but you and I do have both power and authority through Christ. However, authority does no good unless it is exercised, and we do that by letting the devil know that we recognize his works and his lies and that we will not bow down to them. One prayer in Jesus' name is more powerful than the power Satan has.

We are not promised that Satan cannot come against us, but in fact we are told that he can and will do so. However, no permanent harm can come to us. We are guaranteed complete victory, and if we don't see all of it manifested in this life, we will see it in heaven. Paul said that at present we don't see total victory but we do see Jesus (see Heb. 2:8–9).

We have recently formed a habit of saying, "This will end well," while we are waiting for our breakthrough to come in any area. No matter what you are going through now, it will end well! God works all things together for our good, and what Satan means for harm, God intends for good (see Rom. 8:28; Gen. 50:20).

Principalities and Powers

In several places the Bible refers to principalities and powers. These are angels who were created by God, just as Satan was. When Satan rebelled in his pride, refusing to serve God, he was expelled from heaven, and about one-third of the angels who had succumbed to his deception were thrown out with him (see Isa. 14:12–26; Rev. 12:4). Satan and these fallen angels are the principalities and powers, and wickedness in heavenly places that Paul writes about in Ephesians 6:12. They are spirit beings; therefore, they cannot be seen with the natural eye, but their influence and effects can be seen and felt.

When the Bible says the principalities and powers dwell in heavenly places (see Eph. 3:10), it does not refer to heaven as we think of it, where God's throne is and where we will spend eternity. It is the atmosphere between heaven and earth. The demonic forces dwell there, and from there they seek to rule the earth. They appear to have access to the earth and to the people on the earth from the standpoint of influencing their thoughts and actions.

There is a hierarchy among these beings. Some are more powerful than others and may rule over entire cities or nations. We find an interesting account of how these evil spirits operate in Daniel 10. Daniel had been praying for twenty-one days, asking God for understanding about a vision he had seen, but no answer had come yet. This account shows the value of being persistent in prayer. Daniel did not give up and he did get an answer. An angel appeared to Daniel and told him the following.

> Then he said to me, "Do not be afraid, Daniel, for from the first day that you set your heart on understanding this and on humbling yourself before your God, your words were heard, and I have come in response to your words. But the prince of the kingdom of Persia was standing in opposition to me for twenty-one days. Then, behold, Michael, one of the chief [of the celestial] princes, came to help me, for I had been left there with the kings of Persia."
>
> Daniel 10:12–13

From this account it appears that a wicked evil spirit referred to as a principality and power was ruling over Persia, where Daniel lived. God sent an answer to Daniel's prayer the first day he prayed, but this evil entity was strong enough to prevent the angel from delivering the response. As Daniel continued to pray, God sent Michael, one of the archangels (more powerful angels), to deal with the evil principality, and as a result, the first angel was able to get through to Daniel with the answer he sought.

Satan was created as an archangel named Lucifer (see Isa. 14:12 NKJV); he was very beautiful and God loved him greatly. As I mentioned, he was very powerful, which caused him to become prideful, and he rebelled against God. He was thrown out of heaven, but retained his power and now attempts to use it to control the world's system and the people in the world.

Millions of people are not even aware that Satan exists; many others, although they are aware of his existence, do not know they have authority to resist him. They know they have problems, but they don't know what the true problem is. Satan distracts them by injecting thoughts into their minds, urging them to blame other people and even God for their problems.

We War Not with Flesh and Blood

Paul begins Ephesians 6:12 by saying that we war not with flesh and blood, "but against the rulers, against the powers, against the world forces of this [present] darkness, against the spiritual forces of wickedness in the heavenly (supernatural) places." If our warfare (problem) is not with flesh and blood, then who is it with? Obviously, our problems are instigated by the devil and his demons. They definitely can and do work through people and circumstances to frustrate us, cause worry and anxiety, and lead to the loss of peace and joy.

> We waste a great deal of time being angry and fighting with people when we should realize that our war is spiritual, not physical.

We waste a great deal of time being angry and fighting with people when we should realize that our war is spiritual, not physical. We often need to deal with people or circumstances, but if we never realize the truth about the force working through them, we will never truly win. We might win a few battles, but we will not win the war!

Paul taught the Corinthians that the weapons of our warfare are not physical weapons of flesh and blood, but our weapons are divinely powerful for the destruction of strongholds (see 2 Cor. 10:4). Our enemies are not made of flesh and blood, and the weapons we are given to fight them are not flesh and blood, either. Since that is the case, they must be spiritual. We have been given spiritual weapons to fight spiritual enemies. God has not left us helpless in our warfare. He has provided us with weapons and armor, which I will write more about later.

Our main and most helpful spiritual weapon is the Word of God. Other weapons are the name of Jesus, the blood of Christ, continuing to be a blessing and helping others in your times of trial, obedience to God, and praise and worship. We should remember at this point how Jehoshaphat and his army won their battle with worship (see 2 Chron. 20).

Weapons are what we go after the enemy with; they are offensive tools. We speak the name of Jesus, believing in the power that is in that name. We remind the devil of the blood of Christ that defeated him when Jesus died and rose from the dead. We speak the Word of God. We overcome evil with good. We are promptly obedient to God. We worship God and sing His praises. And we do all of this while we are hurting or struggling, in a battle. Doing what is right when everything is going right for us is good, but doing right when all is going wrong for us is a powerful weapon that ultimately defeats the devil.

The problem we run into is the temptation to stop doing the thing we should be doing while we are hurting and to isolate ourselves in our pain and misery, all the while feeling sorry for ourselves and blaming people and circumstances for our problems.

To blame is to assign responsibility for a wrong. We blame people more than anything else. It usually doesn't occur to us that we may have actually caused the problem ourselves by opening a door for Satan, meaning that we allowed him access to our lives. We can open doors to him through disobedience to God, being unforgiving toward those who have hurt us, staying angry, and in many other ways. While it is true that Satan is the force behind all warfare, we must take our part of the responsibility by asking God to reveal to us anything we may have done to open the door for the problems we encounter.

For example, if we are pressured because of debt or financial problems, we may have opened a door through a lack of wisdom in handling our money. The pressure comes from the devil, but we gave him opportunity by not using wisdom and being good stewards over what God has given us.

Locating and taking responsibility for any way we have given the devil an opportunity to harass us is the wise thing to do. God always offers us the opportunity to repent, and He will help us. The apostle James writes that anyone who asks for wisdom during trials gets it from God without reproach or faultfinding (see James 1:5). We don't get help by always blaming someone else for our problems. Even if someone else did cause us problems, the only way out of them is to take responsibility, ask for God's help, and not waste our time being angry and resentful.

It is also possible that we have done nothing to open the door for Satan to attack us. I like to say that there are two times when the devil will attack us—when we are doing something wrong and when we are doing something right.

In Mark 4:15, Jesus says plainly that when the seed of God's Word is planted in our hearts, Satan immediately attempts to steal it. He does so by bringing trouble or persecution, hoping we will fall away from God. Or he may bring a heavy barrage of worries and cares. He also attempts to distract us with worldly pleasures or with the deceitfulness and false security of wealth or fame. So we certainly can see that Satan's attacks aren't always due to something we do wrong; they may also come because we are making progress in our relationship with God and he wants to stop it.

The ways and reasons Satan gains access to us are varied, and we cannot discuss all of them at this time. The main thing we must remember is that Satan is the true source of our problems, and if we just try to deal with the problem and don't deal with the devil, our efforts will be useless.

CHAPTER 10
Dressed for Battle

Put on the whole armor of God, that you may be able to stand against the schemes of the devil.

Ephesians 6:11 ESV

We are in a spiritual war, but, as stated in the last chapter, we have effective weapons with which to fight. In addition to our weapons, we also have armor. God gives us this armor to protect ourselves in battle, but simply having it is not enough—we are instructed to put it on. The term *put on* is used several times in God's Word, and it is an action phrase. It requires us to do something. When I go to my closet each morning, my clothes don't jump off the rack and onto my body. I carefully select them and then I put them on. I check in the mirror to see if I think they look right on me, and if they don't, I change clothes.

I think you will see in this chapter that too often Christians are not wearing their armor. Even worse, they sometimes "wear" behavior and attitudes that don't look good on them at all. For instance, a complaining attitude doesn't look good on someone who is a representative of Christ, yet many Christians regularly complain. A bitter, resentful, and unforgiving attitude doesn't look good on Christians, but far too many have that attitude. These attitudes actually open a door for the devil rather than protect us against him. But God has given us armor, and if we know what it is and make sure we are wearing it all the time, Satan will be much less successful in his attacks against us.

Ephesians 6:14–18 lists the seven things that God considers our armor:

1. Truth
2. Righteousness
3. Peace
4. Faith
5. The Helmet of Salvation
6. The Word of God
7. Prayer

Prior to the mention of each piece of armor, we find the phrase "put on," or another specific action we must take: *Tighten* the belt of truth around your waist, *put on* the breastplate of righteousness, *strap on your feet* the shoes of peace, *lift up* the shield of faith, *take* the helmet of salvation, *wield* the sword of the Spirit, which is the Word of God, and *pray* about everything at all times. We are not automatically protected from the wiles of the devil simply because we are believers in Christ. We must exercise our authority, and putting on the armor is one way we do it.

Since the armor is invisible, one might ask, "How do I put on something I cannot see?" The armor is spiritual and functions to protect us in the spiritual war. The way to put it on is by faith. Believe you have these powerful pieces of armor and walk in obedience to each of the principles they represent.

The Belt of Truth

God's Word is truth, and we are instructed when in battle to tighten the belt of truth around our waist. In other words, hang on to your faith in God's Word firmly when the devil is attacking you with his lies and deceits. The Word of God tells us that some people have no roots, and when trouble comes, they fall away from their faith in God (see Mark 4:16–17). We need to be deeply planted in the Word of God and firmly convinced of its validity so that even in times of intense trouble we won't change our minds and begin to doubt what we believe in good times.

This will require living beyond how we feel or even what we think, but by what we know in our hearts to be true. Each of us will have times when what we believe will be tested, and it is important for us to pass those tests. Each time we do, the devil realizes more and more that he is losing his grip on us and that he is indeed a defeated foe.

> *Each of us will have times when what we believe will be tested, and it is important for us to pass those tests.*

The Breastplate of Righteousness

We have been given right standing with God through our faith in Jesus (see Rom. 5:17). Jesus took our sins and gave us His righteousness (see 2 Cor. 5:21). We need to believe this truth and refuse to live under the guilt and condemnation of sins for which we have repented and received forgiveness.

Jesus not only bore our iniquities, He also bore the guilt and the consequences of them (see Isa. 53:11). If our sins are forgiven and forgotten, according to God's Word, why should we continue to feel guilty about them? God has wiped them away and forgotten them.

However, guilt is a huge problem for many people, and it keeps us feeling pressed down and weak. Satan delights in accusing the believer of many faults and errors. He knows that if he can keep us feeling guilty and condemned, we will feel weak and ineffective in doing God's work, and that just makes us miserable.

For years, guilt was one of my biggest problems. Because of being sexually abused by my father, I grew up always thinking something was wrong with me and feeling guilty about the things that he told me we had to hide. He tried to tell me that what he was doing to me was a good thing, but at the same time, I had to always keep it a secret. This was confusing to me, and I ended up feeling guilty and responsible for what he was doing.

Children don't have the ability to examine an adult's wrong conduct and think, *You have a problem.* They take it upon themselves because it is easy for the devil to make them think any problem is their fault. I have heard, for example, that when parents divorce, most children think it is their fault and that if they would have been better, Mom and Dad would still be together. Satan loves to firmly fix wrong thinking in a child. If he makes us believe lies when we are young, we may function with this deception throughout our lives unless we are blessed to learn the Word of God and actually apply it to our lives.

I carried feelings of guilt until I was well into my forties and was only delivered from it by studying and restudying God's Word on righteousness. We are not, and never will be, righteous in ourselves. God despises self-righteousness, but we are made righteous through faith in Jesus because He gives us His very own right standing with God.

Knowing who we are in Christ is imperative if we are to defeat the devil. If he can keep us feeling guilty and condemned, he rules over us, but knowing who we are in Christ makes us strong and gives us an advantage over the enemy. He may tell us countless lies about ourselves, all negative things he wants us to believe, but knowing the truth of our identity in Christ keeps us walking in truth and defeating the lies of the devil. To know that we are the righteousness of God in Christ means that even though we don't do everything right, we are still viewed as being right with God through our faith. We are not condemned by our faults, but we are thankful when God reveals them because that means we can work with the Holy Spirit, who seeks to set us free and strengthen us.

> *To know that we are the righteousness of God in Christ means that even though we don't do everything right, we are still viewed as being right with God through our faith.*

The Shoes of Peace

We have discussed the importance of peace in an earlier chapter, but I like the idea of putting on our shoes of peace, because we put on our shoes in order to walk around and not injure ourselves. This biblical truth lets us know that if we stay in peace, then no matter what our circumstances, the devil has no power over us. Our natural inclination when trouble comes is to become upset, to be emotional and begin behaving according to how we feel. But that is exactly what God doesn't want us to do. He encourages us to remain peaceful. By doing so we can sense what He is leading us to do in order to overcome our circumstances. Not only will we be able to hear from God, but if the devil cannot upset or frighten us, then he will go away and wait for another opportunity to gain access into our lives.

The devil never just decides to leave us alone and not come

against us or try to deceive us. We must be ready to stand against him at all times. Remember what Peter said: The devil "prowls around like a roaring lion [fiercely hungry], seeking someone to devour" (1 Pet. 5:8).

Paul wrote to the Philippians that not being frightened in any situation would be a clear sign and proof to their opponents of their destruction, and a sign to them of their salvation from God (see Phil. 1:28). In other words, if we stay in peace, then Satan knows he cannot control us, and that releases God to defeat the devil on our behalf because we have shown that our faith is in Him.

> If we stay in peace, then Satan knows he cannot control us.

The Bible says a great deal about the value of peace in spiritual warfare. This is something that we should pray about and strive to maintain with God's help. Remember, fear gets us upset, but faith keeps us calm.

The Shield of Faith

We are instructed to *lift up* the shield of faith. I emphasize this because simply having faith isn't enough; we also need to release our faith in God in order to see it work on our behalf. We can release our faith through *praying, saying,* and *doing.* What I mean is that prayer offered in true faith is a covering over our lives, and it is one of our best defenses against the plots and strategies of the devil. What we say is also very important. Angels obey the voice of God's Word (see Ps. 103:20); they don't listen to us nor are they moved to help us when we complain or speak words of fear, doubt, and unbelief. We are told to hold fast our confession of faith (see Heb. 10:23) during times of trouble and distress.

When we are hurting or frightened, we are tempted to say many negative things and vent our feelings through words, but these are times when we need to be most careful. Jesus was always careful with His words, and even in His time of greatest agony He did not speak negatively. This may be one of our biggest challenges in life, but we should work toward it and regularly see improvement in this area. It requires discipline, self-control, and lots of help from the Holy Spirit. I urge you to pray daily about the words of your mouth. It is part of my regular prayers, and a Scripture I like to pray is Psalm 19:14: "Let the words of my mouth and the meditation of my heart be acceptable in your sight, O LORD, my rock and my redeemer" (ESV).

Our actions also release our faith. Genuine faith always obeys God. As the apostle James said, faith without works is dead, devoid of power (see James 2:17). Faith can be seen or released only as we take action based on what we say we believe. I can pray for a job if I need one, but I also have to look for a job. I can pray for an increase in finances, but I also need to be faithful in giving to God's work and helping people in need.

The Helmet of Salvation

We are told to put on the helmet of salvation. I believe this means to think like people who know they have been born again, who know they are God's children, and who know who they are in Christ. When we are going through trials and difficulties, our temptation is to dwell on many negative thoughts. The devil uses these times to fill our minds with thoughts that make the situation worse instead of better if we take them as our own and meditate on them. Be watchful about your thoughts at all times, but especially in hard times.

I suggest that you not merely resist negative thinking, but take the extra step and purposely think thoughts that will help you in your battle. For example, you can think thoughts such as, *This thing I am going through will end well*, or, *God will work this out for my good*, or, *Today I am going to have a breakthrough—I am expecting something good to happen today*. If we are going to think anything, it may as well be something helpful. Think hopeful, happy thoughts.

The Word of God

Paul's instruction is to take the sword of the Spirit, which is the Word of God. We are to remind the devil of what God says about our situation. When the devil tempted Jesus for forty days and nights in the wilderness, each time the devil told Him a lie, Jesus responded, "It is written...," and He quoted a Scripture that refuted the lie (see Matt. 4:1–11). We should do likewise. God said, "Let him who has my word speak my word faithfully" (Jer. 23:28 ESV).

God's Word is referred to as the sword of the Spirit. As we speak the Word, it is like we are wielding a sword, using it to protect ourselves and attack our enemy, the devil. Satan hates to be reminded of God's promises.

> *Satan hates to be reminded of God's promises.*

Prayer

Paul's last instruction regarding the armor of God is to cover everything with prayer. He says we are to pray "at all times [on every occasion and in every season]," and to that end we are to be watchful and keep alert (see Eph. 6:18). Remember, prayer is one of the most powerful privileges we have been given. At any moment you and I can call for God's help and be assured that He will answer.

We should pray for other people who are in need or fighting battles. They need the strength our prayers give them, just as we need the strength of the prayers of our friends and family. Intercession, or standing in the gap for someone, is one of the greatest ministries God gives all of us. We are all called to intercede on behalf of those in need. Paul understood this and regularly asked the churches to pray for him.

Start your day with prayer and continue throughout the day. Talk to God all the time about everything.

The armor of God is spiritual, yet it is very practical. Each morning we can remind ourselves of these seven pieces of armor and make sure we have each of them in place. We can ask ourselves:

- Am I believing and walking in the truth?
- Do I see myself as the righteousness of God in Christ?
- Am I walking in peace?
- Am I living by faith by praying, saying, and doing God's Word in all areas of my life?
- Am I thinking like a child of God?
- Am I regularly studying and speaking God's Word?
- Have I developed the habit of praying my way through the day?

It is easy to get so caught up in the battle that we worry instead of praying and begin to think negative thoughts instead of the ones God wants us to think. It is also easy to speak negatively out of our emotions or to start feeling guilty, thinking our problems are coming from some sin we have committed. We may have opened a door for the enemy through sin, but we can close it just as quickly as we opened it by repenting of sin. God is not the author of our problems—the devil is, and we should always remember that.

You would never go out of your house without your clothes on (at least I hope you wouldn't), and neither should we go out undressed spiritually. I spend a great deal of time each morning getting dressed in something that looks good on me and fixing my hair and makeup, and many of you do, too. Perhaps if we spent equal time getting dressed spiritually, we would have less trouble with the devil because he wouldn't be able to get to us.

The armor of God is a package of wonderful gifts God has supplied and all we need to do is put them on. God has not left us defenseless in this world to battle on our own with no help. The Holy Spirit is our Helper, and He never leaves us or forsakes us. He will show us what to do in each situation if we will listen and stand in faith while we're waiting for our breakthrough; but we don't always get immediate deliverance. As Paul said, "Put on the complete armor of God, so that you will be able to [successfully] resist and stand your ground in the evil day [of danger], and having done everything [that the crisis demands], to stand firm [in your place, fully prepared, immovable, victorious]" (Eph. 6:13). While you are standing firm, be sure not to take off your armor.

No one but God knows the exact time of your deliverance, but it will come at just the right moment. In the meanwhile, you are gaining experience that will make you stronger for the future. Isaiah wrote that we should not fear, because God will use our difficulties to turn us into new, sharp threshing machines, and we will crush the mountains and make them as chaff (see Isa. 41:15). I don't know about you, but I like the sound of that.

Going through difficulty is not much fun, but keeping our

eyes on the prize gives us strength to endure. Knowing that we have the victory and living in God's peace are blessings that God wants us to enjoy. Not only can we know that we are more than conquerors while the battle still rages, but the devil knows it, too.

The Lion

A story I found from an unknown author makes an important point about spiritual warfare:

> Two explorers were on a jungle safari when suddenly a ferocious lion jumped in front of them. "Keep calm," the first explorer whispered. "Remember what we read in that book on wild animals? If you stand perfectly still and look the lion in the eye, he will turn and run."
>
> "Sure," replied his companion. "You've read the book, and I've read the book. But has the lion read the book?"

Yes, the devil who comes as a lion roaring in fierce hunger seeking someone to seize and devour has read the book. He knows the Word of God well, but if we don't know it, his schemes and deceits will defeat us. Reading and studying the Book (the Bible) is one of the best investments of time we can ever make.

CHAPTER 11

Strength for the Battle

Finally, be strong in the Lord and in the strength of his might.

Ephesians 6:10 ESV

The previous chapter dealt with Ephesians 6:11–18 and the spiritual armor God has provided and instructed us to put on in order to be properly dressed for battle. But if we don't understand the significance of Ephesians 6:10, the verse just before that passage, we will discover that no matter what we put on or try to use to fight our battles with, nothing will work!

I love the Amplified Bible version of this verse:

> In conclusion, be strong in the Lord [draw your strength
> from Him and be empowered through your union with
> Him] and in the power of His [boundless] might.

Our strength is in Christ. He is in us and we are in Him. We draw our strength from Him as we live in close, intimate relationship with Him. The word *union*, which is used in the Amplified Bible, means "oneness." We become one with Christ through our faith in and fellowship with Him. The apostle John writes about the importance of "abiding" in Christ, and that means "living, dwelling, and remaining" with Him (see John 15:5–11). In other words, God's strength doesn't merely come to those who go to church and believe that God exists and that Jesus is His Son, Who died for our sins. God's strength comes to those who are doing life with Him, in Him, and through Him. They know they can do nothing without Him, and they don't waste their time trying to. Paul said, "In Him we live and move and exist [that is, in Him we actually have our being]" (Acts 17:28). That doesn't sound like a casual relationship, but a very committed and serious one.

I was a Christian for a long, long time before I became a serious, fully committed Christian. As I look back I now realize that the devil was successful in controlling me and my behavior because I had no biblical understanding of him as my real enemy, and I certainly didn't know that divine power was available to me. I believed God was powerful, but I was never taught His power could be mine if I only knew how to receive it.

Ephesians 6:10 deserves an entire chapter dedicated to it in this book because it is the prelude for winning our battles with the enemy. Not one of us, no matter how religious we may be, has the strength to defeat the devil. He is not afraid of us unless we know who we are in Christ. The phrase "in Christ" is seen often in the New Testament, and the apostle Paul uses it frequently in Romans and in the Epistles.

To be "in Christ" means that we believe in Him, but it also means that we do everything in our life *with* and *for* Him. Our strength comes from that kind of relationship. We should not try to live life on our own and then—when we think we have a really big problem—call on God to strengthen us. We need to realize that we can do nothing without Him (see John 15:5). We need Him and we need His strength every moment of every day. We need Him surrounding us with His mighty presence at all times.

God has made supernatural power available to us. The word *strong* is taken from a compound of two Greek words, *en* and *dunamis*, making *endunamoo*. We get our English word *dynamite* from the word *dunamis*, because it means "explosive strength, ability, or power." The two words put together convey the idea of being infused or filled with this amazing power. Not only do we have this power, but we have the authority to use it. Paul is clearly reminding the people that in Christ, they have the power to successfully stand against the principalities and powers that are against them.

If we want to overcome the devil's attacks against us, we must have this power. It is not optional; it is imperative. We ask for it, receive it by faith, rely on it, and refuse to attempt anything without it. We may not feel powerful all the time, but God's power is something we receive through faith, not through feeling. We will see the result of God's power in our lives if we consistently rely on it. We are strong only in the Lord!

Paul wrote to the Philippians that he could do all things through Christ, Who was his strength (see Phil. 4:13). He always made clear that our strength, our power, our ability, and our might come from Christ. We are weak, but He is strong! Paul made that easy to see in 2 Corinthians 12:7–10, when he wrote that God's strength is perfected and "shows itself most effectively" in our weakness. It is only because we are weak that God offers us His strength. If we will humbly remember that without Him we are nothing and can do nothing, but that in Christ we are made strong and can do all things, then we will live effective lives in which the devil's strategies and deceits are not successful against us. He will never give up trying, but as we remain vigilant and watchful, he will not succeed. Remember that in the midst of many difficulties, we are more than conquerors through Christ Who loves us (see Rom. 8:37).

The Greater One Lives in Us

The apostle John writes about the Antichrist (the devil), and all those who do not confess Jesus. He says that we have already overcome them because He Who is in us is greater than he who is in the world, meaning the devil (see 1 John 4:4).

Satan has power; he is intelligent, cunning, crafty, deceptive, determined, and capable. He takes advantage of every opportunity given to him. Our own power and intelligence doesn't come close to matching his, but Christ's power is much greater than his and His Spirit lives in us. The One who is in us is greater than the devil. The One who is for us is greater than the one who is against us.

Satan's power is no match for the power of the Holy Spirit. God never asks us to do anything without giving us the power to do it. He has commanded us to resist and stand firmly against the devil and his demonic forces, and we have what it takes to do it as long as we remember that God is our strength.

Paul teaches us that we are strong in the *power* of His (Christ's) might. The word translated *power* is an important word. It is from the Greek word *kratos*, which is the same word used to describe God raising Jesus from the dead. We have that same power in us! We are told that if the Spirit of Him who raised Christ from the dead dwells in us, it will quicken or give life to our mortal bodies (see Rom. 8:11). The life it gives us is not only the ability to walk around and breathe, but to be powerful and live as more than conquerors.

> *The same power that raised Christ from the dead dwells in you!*

Stop for a moment and just take in this truth: The same power that raised Christ from the dead dwells in you!

Just think of the tomb where Jesus' dead body lay. Consider how dark and cold it must have been. Roman soldiers stood outside guarding it. But on resurrection morning, the mighty, unmatchable, unimaginable, immeasurable power of God came into that dark tomb and filled it with light. God's life flowed into the body that lay there, the tomb blasted open, and the soldiers crumpled to the ground. They lay paralyzed by this mighty power, totally unable to move until Jesus' resurrection was complete.

Now think about it again: This same power dwells in you and me as believers in Christ! It is a power that defeats Satan, changes circumstances, heals sick bodies, and enables us to stand strong through the storms of life. It enables us to do anything we need to do, and it is available to us in unlimited supply.

Be Strength-Minded

No matter what is ours in Christ, if we don't believe it is ours, it does us no practical good. As we have already established, our thoughts are very important. They prepare us for action. I have known many weak-minded people in my life and at times my life has been adversely affected by some of those people. They believed they could not do things and therefore they did not try. My mother did not believe she could face the scandal of having people know my father was sexually abusing me, so she stayed with him and hid from the truth. Her weakness hurt my brother and me, and it destroyed her chance to have a good life herself. By not confronting my father, she enabled him to keep hurting people.

Sadly, the world is filled with people who are weakness-minded. Most are unbelievers, but many are believers who do not yet know who they are in Christ and Who He is in them.

We should be strength-minded. Remind yourself every day,

and several times a day if needed, that you are strong in the Lord and in the power of His might. That the greater one is alive in you, and His strength is made perfect in your weakness. Say out loud several times a day, *"I am strong in the Lord."*

I love the Amplified Bible Classic Edition version of Philippians 4:13, which says we are "ready for anything and equal to anything" through Christ. Let your thinking be *I can do whatever I need to do in life through Christ*. Paul tells us that we are more than conquerors through Him Who loves us and that nothing can separate us from that love (see Rom. 8:37–39). I believe that being more than a conqueror means you know you have victory before the battle ever begins. This means that you believe and fill your mind with thoughts of strength, power, ability, and might. It is full of "can do" thinking, not "can't do" thinking.

If you will form a habit of being strength-minded, it will prepare you for whatever comes your way in life. Not every storm is in the forecast, and we need to live ready for each one—not simply try to get ready when we are already in the heat of battle.

In addition to the Scripture verses I have already mentioned, here are a few others you should learn and meditate on regularly to help you become strength-minded. As you fill your mind with these, instead of seeing yourself as weak, incapable, unable, and unsure, you will see yourself as strong in Christ and able to do what needs to be done. This new thinking will add enthusiasm to your life, and you will feel on top of things rather than under all of the trials and anxieties of the world.

- "He gives strength to the weary, and to him who has no might He increases power" (Isa. 40:29).
- "But those who wait for the LORD [who expect, look for, and hope in Him] will gain new strength and renew their power;

they will lift up their wings [and rise up close to God] like eagles [rising toward the sun]; they will run and not become weary, they will walk and not grow tired" (Isa. 40:31).

- "Do not fear [anything], for I am with you; do not be afraid, for I am your God. I will strengthen you, be assured I will help you" (Isa. 41:10).
- "But the Lord is faithful, and He will strengthen you [setting you on a firm foundation] and will protect and guard you from the evil one" (2 Thess. 3:3).

I cannot stress enough the importance of thinking about these Scriptures and similar ones on a regular basis. Don't miss even one day thinking and saying, "I am strong in the Lord and in the power of His might" (see Eph. 6:10). Keep your mind renewed with the Word of God; otherwise, worldly thinking will slowly creep in and the devil will fill your mind with *I can't* and *I'm not* thoughts.

We do not have the power to do whatever we want to do, but we do have the power to do what God wants us to do if we will only believe it.

Unless we are first strengthened with God's power, it is useless to try to put on, let alone keep on, the armor of God mentioned in Ephesians 6:11–18.

Your Authority as a Believer

We not only have *power* through our union with Christ, but we also have been given the *authority* to use it. All power in heaven and on earth has been given to Jesus, and He has given it to us (see Matt. 28:18–20). We are not just waiting to get His power someday; it has been given to us, and we need to believe we have it.

God created us to be the head and not the tail, above and not beneath (see Deut. 28:13). God created us to rule, not to be enslaved and ruled over. In the Garden of Eden, He gave Adam and Eve authority over the animals and the Garden, telling them to be fruitful and multiply and to tend the Garden. He also told them to subdue the earth (see Gen. 1:27–28).

When Jesus sent His disciples out to minister, He gave them the right to exercise power and authority over all demons and to heal diseases (see Luke 9:1). We can be assured that God will never send us out to do anything without giving us both the power and authority to do it.

Some of the words used to describe authority are *dominance*, *jurisdiction*, and *control*. Authority is also the right to give orders or make decisions, and it is a quality that gives a person confidence. God's Word tells us that we already have and now possess this power and authority (see Luke 10:19), and we should behave as though we believe it.

For example, we should walk with our heads up, not hanging down. We should look directly at people when talking with them, and we should speak in a clear voice and not mumble. It is easy to spot someone who feels insignificant and weak; they have a certain demeanor about them that indicates a lack of confidence. But we can also recognize those who are confident, who know who they are, and who believe they can do what needs to be done in any situation.

We are God's representatives in the earth and we should behave as such, especially when it comes to dealing with the devil and his demons. We are not to be fearful, lacking confidence, weak-minded, and doubtful. It is time to realize that we have power and authority.

Jesus told His disciples that all authority in heaven and on earth had been given to Him, and then He commanded them to go and make disciples of all nations (see Matt. 28:18–20). The obvious inference in these verses is that He is transferring His authority to them so they can obey His instructions.

Paul writes that God the Father has put all things in subjection under Christ's feet, and appointed Him supreme head of all things in the church, which is His body (see Eph. 1:22–23). Christ is the Head, and we believers are considered His body because we are the ones walking the earth and being the hands and feet of Jesus. We are doing in His name the work He began while He was here on Earth. If all things are under His feet, then they are under our feet because we are His body. The knowledge of these spiritual truths should give us a quiet yet powerful confidence that enables us to resist all opposition and do mighty things in Jesus' name and for His glory.

Ask yourself how you feel and what you believe about these things you are reading. Are you confident, courageous, not easily defeated, determined, and bold? Are you strength-minded? Do you believe you can do all things through Christ who is your strength? Do you see yourself as someone with authority, someone who is the head and not the tail?

If you see yourself the way God sees you, each day can be an exciting adventure, even if your day is ordinary. As believers in Christ, with His power and authority, we can live ordinary life in an extraordinary way. The authority we have gives us the ability to have peace in the midst of the storm, joy in difficult circumstances, and certainty when everything around us is shaking.

> *As believers in Christ, with His power and authority, we can live ordinary life in an extraordinary way.*

I pray you will see yourself in a brand-new way. Hold your head up high and go through life expecting good things to happen to you and through you. Just one person who understands who they are in Christ can change the world for the better, and you can be one who does it. You are significant to God's plan, and you have all the authority you need!

CHAPTER 12

The Importance of Watchfulness

Be sober-minded; be watchful. Your adversary the devil prowls around like a roaring lion, seeking someone to devour.

1 Peter 5:8 ESV

A watchful person is someone who is alert and keeps an attentive eye on things. For example, a watchful driver quickly sees and stops for pedestrians crossing the street. A person who is watchful over his finances will not get into oppressive debt and end up not being able to pay his bills. As we walk through this world, it pays to be watchful in all areas, and it especially pays to watch out for the devil so he doesn't slither into our lives and deceive us. There is almost no limit to the ways—both big and little—the devil conspires to ruin God's work and attack His people. He desires and works hard to bring Christians into bondage and unhappiness.

John Bunyan's book *The Pilgrim's Progress* was published in 1678. Bunyan wrote it to help believers understand what they would face and know how to be watchful and overcome the enemy. This allegorical story about how Christians can make progress in their walk with God presents a clear picture of the wiles of the devil and depicts a man who has repented of his sin and received Christ as his Savior. But his troubles do not end there.

Teaching people that once they are saved their troubles are over is a huge mistake. I often tell people who accept Christ in my conferences that becoming a child of God does not mean they will never have any more problems. It does mean, however, that they will never have to fight their battles alone. I also tell them that their worst day with Jesus will be better than their best day ever was without Him.

A few great books similar to *The Pilgrim's Progress* have been written on the subject of the soul's conflict after salvation, but according to D. Martyn Lloyd-Jones, most of them were written before 1880. This type of literature was characteristic of the Puritan era, but little has been produced since then—not nearly enough to equip Christians for the battle we are in. John Bunyan called it the "Holy War," and Richard Sibbes called it the "Soul's Conflict." Today, we refer to it as "spiritual warfare."

I have been greatly blessed personally by portions of a more recent book that has helped me, which is Watchman Nee's *The Spiritual Man*, because it thoroughly deals with the subject of the soul and the conflict we experience as we mature in Christ.

We need writing and teaching on the wiles of the devil and especially about the ways he attempts to afflict believers. If we are forewarned, then we can be forearmed. If we understand how the enemy comes against us and if we know how to resist him, we can be ready to combat his attacks instead of taken by surprise and defeated. This is one reason I have written this book.

The Old Testament tells a story about how God led the children of Israel to the Promised Land by a much longer route than necessary.

> So it happened, when Pharaoh let the people go, God did
> not lead them by way of the land of the Philistines, even

though it was nearer; for God said, "The people might change their minds when they see war [that is, that there will be war], and return to Egypt."

Exodus 13:17

I have always found this interesting, and I believe God is telling us through this story that we can expect opposition when we begin to take His promises personally. For this reason, God often has to lead us into all He has promised us through a long or difficult way. As a result we grow in the knowledge of who we are in Christ, realize that we do have authority over the enemy, and learn how to recognize and resist his tactics.

Satan loves for us to be ignorant, and ignorance is all we are left with if we have no knowledge. People perish for a lack of knowledge (see Hosea 4:6), but God wants us well-informed. I urge you to search for information that will help prepare you to stand firm in battle and know that God will fight for you.

God knows that if we are fearful and turn back every time life becomes difficult, we will never possess what Jesus died to give us. So He works with us and teaches us to know our enemy and to be assured that he may come against us one way, but will flee from us seven ways (see Deut. 28:7). We need confidence in God, and that only comes as we experience His deliverance. Each time we have a problem and we trust God and see victory, we become a little bit stronger and Satan's wiles affect us less the next time he attacks. I remind you again that we do not war against flesh and blood. Our war is not against people, or against our circumstances, but against Satan, the true source of all misery.

Live Carefully

Paul exhorts us to "walk carefully" (see Eph. 5:15), which means to live watchfully against temptation and evil. Other biblical phrases with meanings similar to that of *watchful* include "be alert," "don't sleep," and "be on guard." Numerous Scriptures instruct us to pay close attention to what is going on and that is because we have a formidable, crafty, deceptive enemy who has plans for our destruction. I am fond of Ephesians 5:15–17, and I believe we need to take time to look at it carefully.

> Therefore see that you walk carefully [living life with honor, purpose, and courage; shunning those who tolerate and enable evil], not as the unwise, but as wise [sensible, intelligent, discerning people], making the very most of your time [on earth, recognizing and taking advantage of each opportunity and using it with wisdom and diligence], because the days are [filled with] evil. Therefore do not be foolish and thoughtless, but understand and firmly grasp what the will of the Lord is.

At times we may become lazy or passive about our watchfulness, especially concerning spiritual things. Although we have learned spiritual truths, we must keep our knowledge fresh. This is why Paul encourages us to "stand fast therefore in the liberty" we have gained in Christ and not to be ensnared again in the "yoke of bondage" from which we have been set free (see Gal. 5:1 NKJV). His meaning is clear: We can gain freedom and

> *Although we have learned spiritual truths, we must keep our knowledge fresh.*

be watchful for a period of time, but if we are not careful, we become sleepy or inactive and find ourselves in bondage once again.

For example, we know to be careful about our thoughts and words, yet at times we are tempted to think and speak in ways that are not in line with God's Word because we do not realize that Satan is the source of such thoughts and words. I experience attacks on my mind just as everyone does, and I have prayed that the Holy Spirit will make me aware when thoughts from the devil enter my mind. When He does, if I am by myself I say, "No, Satan, you are a liar and I don't receive that thought." If I'm not in a place where I can speak aloud, I resist quietly and he goes away to wait for a time to try again.

We all wish we could get to the point where we do not have to deal with the devil, but that will not happen as long as we are on the earth. The enemy fought Jesus until the very end, and he will do the same with us. Resisting Satan doesn't have to be hard work. I think we can actually learn to enjoy recognizing his wiles quickly, knowing we have authority and power to resist him.

I sleep very soundly at night, and sometimes our son comes to our house very late to use our exercise equipment. He has told me often, "I came in and did all kinds of things and you never even knew I was here. It's a good thing I wasn't a burglar because I could have carried off half the house and you wouldn't have known it."

That's the way it is if we are not watchful against the enemy. He comes into our lives and robs us, and we don't even recognize what is happening. We need to wake up and live more carefully.

As D. Martyn Lloyd-Jones wrote in *The Christian Warfare*, one of the greatest deficits of the church is teaching about the wiles and deception of the devil. He is our enemy, but God will fight our battles alongside us if we do our part. Some people would rather not hear about the devil, but that is a mistake. We don't have to be excessive in our teaching and study in this area, but neither should we ignore it.

If we lack knowledge in this area, we will not be prepared when the enemy does attack. Jesus' parable of the ten virgins in Matthew 25:1–13 teaches us what happens when we are not well prepared. All ten virgins took their lamps and went to meet the bridegroom. Five were foolish (thoughtless, silly, and careless), and five were wise. The bridegroom was delayed, and they all fell asleep as they waited for him. When he did come and they awoke, the foolish virgins realized they had not brought any extra oil for their lamps. They had brought only enough oil for everything to go perfectly, according to their plan, and no more. They were like people who never plan for heavy traffic when they are going somewhere, and they frequently arrive late to their appointments.

The foolish virgins went to the wise virgins and asked for some of their oil, but the wise had to say no so they would not run out of oil themselves. How sad the foolish virgins must have been because they were not wise and watchful. They were too lazy to prepare properly and missed out on a blessing.

Lazy people often run to active people and want them to give them what they worked hard for, but that is not God's way. We all have equal opportunity. God gives us what we need to work with, but if we won't do the work, then we miss out.

The parable ends with these strong words of advice: "Therefore, be on the alert [be prepared and ready], for you do not know the day nor the hour [when the Son of Man will come]" (Matt. 25:13).

This parable obviously refers to the return of our Lord and makes the point that we should stay active and be ready for His coming at all times. But we can also apply this principle to being watchful against the enemy: If we don't stay prepared, he will sneak in and rob us of the good life Jesus purchased for us with His blood.

Watch and Pray

When Jesus was in the Garden of Gethsemane preparing for the suffering He would soon endure, His disciples kept falling asleep. When Jesus found them sleeping, He said, "So, you men could not stay awake and keep watch with Me for one hour?" (Matt. 26:40). This seems sad, doesn't it, that He was in one of the most difficult times of His life and His own disciples went to sleep?

Jesus said to them as He says to us:

> "Keep actively watching and praying that you may not come into temptation; the spirit is willing, but the body is weak."
>
> Matthew 26:41

Satan was tempting Jesus to run from the suffering. Of course, Jesus did not want to go through the suffering He would soon endure. He asked that the cup of suffering be removed from Him if at all possible, but quickly added, "My Father, if this cannot pass away unless I drink it, Your will be done" (Matt. 26:42).

Jesus knew that during temptation, He had to keep praying, and we must learn that also. As a matter of fact, I have formed a habit of praying regularly for God to strengthen me in areas I know are weaknesses for me. I name them and ask for strength because I don't want to be caught off guard and let the enemy sneak up on me and take advantage of them. This, in addition to praying immediately anytime I feel I am being attacked, helps me win lots of battles, and I encourage you to do the same.

Some people believe Satan's lie that the temptations they face are simply too strong for them to overcome, but that is not true according to God's Word. It tells us that no temptation, no matter what it is or where it comes from, is one we cannot resist. God promises to always provide a way out if we trust in Him and lean on Him. No temptation is beyond our ability to resist, but God is faithful and He will always provide a way out (see 1 Cor. 10:13).

Don't let the devil convince you that you cannot overcome addictions or temptation of any kind, because He that is in you is greater than he that is in the world (see 1 John 4:4). If we believe we cannot conquer a temptation, then we won't be able to do it, but if we believe we can, then we are half-way to victory. After that, we need to remain steadfast, ask God if there is anything we should do, and, if so, then do it. Then we wait patiently for God to bring us victory. While we are waiting, we can be assured that He is working, even though we may not see or feel it.

> If we believe we cannot conquer a temptation, then we won't be able to do it.

In the garden just before His crucifixion, Jesus asked His disciples to stay awake and pray with Him because He knew prayer was the weapon He needed to use at that time. The reason Satan fights so hard against prayer is that prayer is the way to defeat him. Remember that God told Jehoshaphat He would fight his battle for him, but He also told him to take his place, which was one of prayer and worship (see 2 Chron. 20:15–22).

At the end of Paul's discourse about the various pieces of armor God has supplied for us, which we are instructed to "put on," he asked the Ephesians to pray for him that he might continue to speak boldly about the good news of salvation (see Eph. 6:11–19). I cannot imagine what kind of courage it took to preach the gospel in those days. Preachers were continually threatened with death and prison, often enduring beatings, hunger, and many other painful sufferings. Paul knew he needed the strength of the believers' prayers in order to keep going. He was alert and always ready to pray anytime he felt he needed to, and he encouraged all those he taught to be the same way.

Don't assume you are strong in an area just because you have been tested before and passed the test. Always know that your strength comes from the Lord, and He will supply all you need if you will only ask and keep on asking.

The Return of Christ

One of these days Christ will come for us. Our time on this earth will be up and it will be too late to get ready if we are not ready when He comes. We don't want to be like the five foolish virgins who slept and didn't do what they should have done when they should have done it.

Jesus said no one knows the day and hour of His return, not the angels or even the Son of God, but only the Father Himself (see Mark 13:32). The day will come, and for some it may come much quicker than they think. We all plan to live a long life and die at an old age, but that doesn't always happen, and when our time is up here on Earth, there is nothing we can do to change it. Jesus strongly exhorts us to be on guard and constantly alert. I want to quote five verses out of Mark 13 because I am amazed at how frequently Jesus spoke the same words over and over. They must be very important or He would not have done that.

> "Be on guard and stay constantly alert [and pray]; for you
> do not know when the appointed time will come. It is

like a man away on a journey, who when he left home put his servants in charge, each with his particular task, and also ordered the doorkeeper to be continually alert. Therefore, be continually on the alert—for you do not know when the master of the house is coming, whether in the evening, or at midnight, or when the rooster crows, or in the morning—[stay alert,] in case he should come suddenly and unexpectedly and find you asleep and unprepared. What I say to you I say to everyone, 'Be on the alert [stay awake and be continually cautious]!' "

Mark 13:33–37

Satan definitely wants us to be unprepared when Jesus returns for us, and he does everything he can to distract us from pursuing a relationship with the Lord—from prayer, from Bible study, from obediently serving God by helping others, and from many other things that strengthen our walk with God. Therefore, it is urgent that we learn his character, understand how he operates, and take our responsibility so God can effectively fight our battles with and for us.

What Should We Watch For?

First and foremost, we should watch for thoughts that are not in agreement with God's Word, because all the words we speak and the actions we take come from our thoughts. I'll repeat what I often say: "Where the mind goes, the man follows."

> All the words we speak and the actions we take come from our thoughts.

If we are watchful concerning our thoughts, we can cast down wrong ones and purposely choose right ones. By doing so we can completely avoid many miserable days the devil has planned for us.

Be watchful against temptation because Satan is the tempter of all wrongdoing. God tempts us to do good things, and those are the temptations we should *not* resist. Remembering that we overcome evil with good is very important (see Rom. 12:21). If we stay busy doing good, there will not be room for the evil that persistently tries to draw us away from God.

Another thing to watch for is "self," or selfishness, or self-centeredness! In the final analysis, people's greatest battles are with themselves, and I will address this in the next chapter.

CHAPTER 13

"Self"

Let each of you look not only to his own interests, but also to the interests of others.

Philippians 2:4 ESV

Self, in the context in which I want to use it, represents selfishness or being self-centered. The devil tempts and provokes us to want to sin, but self makes the final choice and is therefore responsible when we do sin. When people are being selfish, they oppose God's will by exercising their own will and doing as they please. What they want is more important to them than what God wants. This is what caused the fall of Satan as well as the fall of Adam and Eve (see Isa. 14:12–14; Gen. 3:1–7). God created Satan perfectly, with unusual beauty and faculties. He had amazing abilities and great power. But he fell because of pride, which is nothing more than a manifestation of self. He wasn't satisfied with the amazing gifts and abilities God had bestowed on him; he wanted to be equal to—or above—God. He said that he would lift his throne "above the stars of God" and "ascend above the heights of the clouds" so he could be "like the Most High" (see Isa. 14:13–14). Evil exists in this self, which is found in angelic beings as well as in people.

We know from Scripture that when God cast Satan out of heaven, the angels, who also rebelled against God, were thrown down with him (see Rev. 12:7–9). They were not forced to rebel; they rebelled deliberately. God wants us to love and obey Him because we choose to, not because we have no other choice and are merely programmed to do so. Thus, He gives us free will, which presents us continually with the need to choose between good and evil. Satan tempts us to do evil, and God urges us to do good things.

The choice is always ours. Free will—the right to choose—is a wonderful freedom and a tremendous responsibility. Because we have freedom of choice, we must also take responsibility for the outcomes of our choices. Every choice comes with a consequence, and for that reason God continually urges us in His Word to choose His will so we may end up with a life we will enjoy (see Deut. 30:19).

> *Free will—the right to choose—is a wonderful freedom and a tremendous responsibility.*

Satan, in his plan of attack, constantly plays on the tendency to be selfish, which is in all of us. Throughout the Bible we can easily spot the people who made selfish choices and read about their outcomes. We can also spot the ones who obediently followed God out of love for Him and see what their outcomes were. I often feel that the Bible is a simple message presented over and over in a variety of ways. Its message is that the righteous will flourish and the wicked will meet with ultimate destruction.

I believe God wants us to use our free will to choose His will. When we do, life gets really good. It is not without challenge, but we do continually see the favor of God in our lives, and we ultimately experience deliverance from our trials and difficulties. God will not force us to do the right thing, but He urges us to do so for our own good.

The Disciples

We are surprised at the disciples' selfish behavior as we read about their arguments about which of them was the greatest (see Luke 22:24). To be chosen as one of the twelve disciples was a tremendous privilege, but it seems that no matter what God gives us, we still find a way to think we should have something else. Truly, our greatest battle is with our self. Self is filled with greed. It can be defeated, but only by relying on God, being willing to obey Him, and aggressively giving of ourselves to others and truly desiring their good. To be selfish is natural, but to be unselfish requires effort. The Holy Spirit gives us the strength to do the right thing if that is what we choose.

We may be surprised and disappointed by the disciples' behavior while not recognizing the selfishness in ourselves. Selfishness (self) is an inbred weakness in our flesh due to the fall of man. It will never completely disappear as long as we are on this earth, but we do not have to let it rule us. God has given us many tools with which to fight the enemy of self. First, we can call on His strength at any time and fully expect to receive it. Second, God has given us a spirit of discipline (see 2 Tim. 1:7). And third, we have self-control as a fruit of the Holy Spirit, Who dwells in us (see Gal. 5:22–23). We also should realize that Satan tempts us to be selfish, and when he does, we should resist him.

We are wise to remain aware of how strongly self seeks to rule us. It is stirred up by the devil, and unless we recognize the problem and resist it through the power of God, it will rule over us. I have found the best way to resist being selfish and greedy is to be an aggressive giver in all areas of life. Is it easy? No! Do I fail often? Yes! But thankfully, when we fall God helps us get back up again and resume doing the right thing. When people are determined to do so, they will gain victory over the devil.

It amazes me how selfish I still can be even after forty-three years of studying God's Word, ministering to others, and desiring to live for God. Saying that we want God's will in our lives is easy, but making the quality decision to follow through with right action is more difficult. I can assure you that even while I write this chapter on self, I have been convicted of previously unseen areas of selfishness in myself that I want to confront and intend to do so with God's help.

Asking God to reveal any areas of selfishness in us is a wise course of action. The bottom line is simply that we want what we want and are not naturally inclined to sacrifice our desires for another person's happiness. Doing so requires supernatural help, the help of God. It also requires being willing to suffer in the flesh in order to do God's will. When our flesh doesn't get what it wants, it whines and pouts; it may even get depressed and waste a lot of time wallowing in self-pity. But thankfully, we can resist all of those bad habits through the power of God.

Selfish People Are Unhappy People

I have discovered through personal experience that being selfish and happy at the same time is impossible. God has not created us to live only for ourselves, and when we try to live for self, we miss out on the joy Jesus came to give us.

One of my favorite Scriptures is 2 Corinthians 5:15. It declares that Jesus "died for all, so that all those who live might live no longer to and for themselves, but to and for Him Who died and was raised again for their sake" (AMPC). Yes, Jesus died for our sins. He paid the debt we owed and took the punishment we deserved. He also came to set us free from bondage. The greatest bondage people can endure is to be so selfish that their entire world is filled with themselves, what they want, and what they need. I often say that the greatest thing God has set me free from is "me."

> The greatest thing God has set me free from is "me."

Learning to love others and care about their happiness is the only way to be happy. Why? God has established a law in the earth called sowing and reaping. People will reap whatever they sow—and only what they sow (see Gal. 6:7). If people sow happiness into the lives of others, they will reap happiness for themselves. If we do what benefits and makes another person happy, benefit and happiness will come back to us. However, if we are greedy and self-centered toward others, then we will find only misery. Selfish people are lonely because they are the only ones in their tiny little world.

When Paul wrote, "I have been crucified with Christ; it is no longer I who live, but Christ lives in me" (Gal. 2:20 NKJV), I believe he was saying he was no longer living merely for himself and his own interests, but for what Christ desired of him. I want to mention that Paul penned this Scripture twenty years after his conversion on the Damascus road. I am a bit comforted to know that it took Paul a while to mature spiritually to the point where he could write these words. I believe the same principle is true for most of us. We are so bent on making ourselves happy and getting what we want that it takes time for us to fully realize the only way to get what we desire is to give ourselves to Jesus completely and let Him use us for the benefit of other people.

I don't mean to imply that we don't take care of ourselves or do anything for ourselves, but simply that we should not be filled with self while caring nothing for the needs and desires of others. The principle of sowing and reaping is exciting to me because it means I can give away what I would like to have and be assured that in due time I will reap a harvest according to what I have sown.

If you are unhappy and lack joy, I strongly encourage you to do more for other people, and if you do, I believe you will experience a harvest of joy in your own life.

Self = Pride

The devil loves nothing more than to destroy our witness for Christ by tempting us to be selfish, self-centered, and filled with pride. He tries to make us think more highly of ourselves than we should and to be proud of what we do well without thanking God for enabling us to do it. Pride causes critical judgment toward those who can't do what we can do. That makes us feel superior to them and usually grows into a disdain and disrespect for those we view as not as good as we are. It may also cause us to mistreat them. The way we treat other people is very important to God, and it possibly says more about our character than anything else.

If you are exceptionally intelligent, learn easily, and retain information, or if you are a gifted public speaker or an amazingly talented singer, you did not give yourself those abilities. God gave them to you, and they are to be used to glorify Him, not so you can be puffed up with pride.

For who regards you as superior or what sets you apart as special? What do you have that you did not receive [from another]? And if in fact you received it [from God

or someone else], why do you boast as if you had not
received it [but had gained it by yourself]?

1 Corinthians 4:7

Any ability we have comes from God, so why do we boast?
Simply because the self that is in us wants to feel good; it wants
to be above others, the best, the greatest of all. The only way to
accomplish that is to find someone who isn't as good as we are at
something and use it as an opportunity to feel superior. Those
we belittle in our thoughts and attitudes have abilities we do not
have, and we should applaud what they can do rather than com-
pare ourselves to them.

If you have a good singing voice, do you often find yourself singing a little louder than others in church so you will be
heard and admired? If you have knowledge in many things, do
you find yourself continually offering advice that people do not
ask for? In *The Christian Warfare,* D. Martyn Lloyd-Jones tells
about several men who testified about the sins from which God
had delivered them, and the discussion degenerated into a con-
test about who was the worst sinner! I think that might be the
most ridiculous display of pride I have heard. They were actually
boasting about their sin.

I have noticed when trying to fellowship with groups of minis-
ters that the conversation often becomes a boasting session about
who is doing the most in ministry, how big their ministries are,
how many followers they have on their social media accounts,
and so on. I have caught myself all too often taking part in the
competition and have had to ask God to forgive me for the sin of
pride.

Pride prevents us from being thankful because we think we
deserve what we have and more. Pride causes people to talk

excessively, often about themselves. James writes that we should be slow to speak and quick to hear (see James 1:19).

Pride also causes us to judge others harshly for their sin while thinking, *I would never do that.* But the Bible says we are to be careful when we think we stand firm, "immune to temptation, being overconfident and self-righteous," because we might fall (see 1 Cor. 10:12). How often do we end up doing the same thing for which we have judged someone else? Too often, I think! We always need to remember that the sin of pride is what caused Satan's fall, and we don't want to follow his example.

The Lord Is Coming Soon

> Let all men know and perceive and recognize your unselfishness (your considerateness, your forbearing spirit). The Lord is near [He is coming soon].
>
> Philippians 4:5 AMPC

The Lord will return sooner than most of us may think, and each of us will be required to give an account of our time on earth (see Rom. 14:12). When that time comes, it will be too late to go back and do the things we should have done. Although we don't earn salvation by our works, but only by faith in what Jesus did for us through His death and resurrection, our works are important because they demonstrate our faith and represent our relationship with God.

We are living in a time of great confusion. The devil is actively working through wicked people to try and remove God from everything in our society. As believers in Christ, we must take a strong stand for what is right and let people see Jesus through us. The only way we can do that is to forget about ourselves and let God use us for His glory. We need not worry that if we do so we will live miserable lives and never have anything we desire, because the exact opposite will happen. If we give up focusing on ourselves and trying to please ourselves all the time, and instead ask God to use us to help other people, His blessings will overwhelm us.

> All disobedience is directly linked to selfishness.

All disobedience is directly linked to selfishness. Adam and Eve saw something they wanted in the garden, and even though God prohibited it, they decided to please themselves instead of God (see Gen. 2:16–17; 3:6). The devil tempted Eve to disobey God, but he did not tell her what the consequences of her disobedience would be (see Gen. 3:1–5). He never does, and sadly, we often find out too late that in trying to get everything for ourselves, we have lost what was most important.

How many husbands have spent so much time working to make more money or to climb the ladder of success to build their ego that they have ended up losing their families? Far too many! When you are on your deathbed you will not ask to see your bank balance. You will want to be with family and those who love you.

The Bible tells many stories about people whose selfishness led them into trouble:

- Cain killed Abel because of selfishness (see Gen. 4:8–9; 1 John 3:12).
- Joseph's brothers sold him into slavery and lied to their father because of their selfishness and jealousy (see Gen. 37:18–33; Acts 7:9–10).

- King David committed adultery and murder because of self-ishness (see 2 Sam. 11:2–17).

We cannot find a sin that was or is not committed because of self. We all have to deal with it, but we do not have to let it win the battle. If we are willing to die to self, as God's Word instructs us, we can be freed from its tyranny.

> "I assure you and most solemnly say to you, unless a grain of wheat falls into the earth and dies, it remains alone [just one grain, never more]. But if it dies, it produces much grain and yields a harvest."
>
> John 12:24

Jesus laid aside His self and died for us. Because of that, a great harvest of souls has been saved who will spend eternity in Heaven. The same principle works in our lives. If we are willing to die to self, God can use us to work in His Kingdom and lead others to a saving knowledge of Christ through our words and behavior.

The apostle Paul, inspired by the Holy Spirit, writes that we should consider ourselves to be dead to sin, but alive to God. He urges us not to let sin reign in our mortal bodies or obey its lusts and passions. He tells us not to continue offering our bodies to sin as instruments of wickedness, but by a decisive act, to offer them to God as instruments of righteousness. Once we have done that, and as we continue doing it, sin will no longer be a master over us (see Rom. 6:11–14).

Thoughts and Emotions

Our thoughts and emotions are filled with self, and if we intend to live for God, we cannot allow either of them to rule over us. We will always contend with them, but we can learn to live beyond them. I may feel like being angry with someone who has treated me unjustly, but I can choose to forgive that person as God instructs me to do.

I may think I simply must have something and will have to compromise my integrity in order to get it, but I can cast down that wrong thought and decide to do what is right no matter what my carnal thoughts tell me. We have a mind of the flesh and a mind of the spirit. Choosing to obey the mind of the flesh ends in misery of every kind, but choosing to follow the mind of the spirit ends in life and peace and spiritual well-being—both now and forever! (See Romans 8:5–6.)

Although Satan works hard to use the weakness of self against us, he cannot win if we are determined to follow God rather than self. The Bible frequently instructs us to face ourselves honestly and to seek the truth at all times. We are wise to examine ourselves often to see if we are living under the control of self or under the control of the Holy Spirit. We don't examine ourselves in order to condemn ourselves for our faults, but in order to recognize them, repent of them, and receive God's help to overcome them.

CHAPTER 14

Stand Still and See the Salvation of the Lord

What we run from hurts us the most.

author unknown

In Exodus 14:13, Moses gave the Israelites an instruction that would be life-changing for them if they would follow it—to "stand still, and see the salvation of the LORD" (NKJV). They had been in slaves in Egypt for four hundred years, and freedom was finally within reach. Pharaoh had reluctantly let the people go into the wilderness, and God had told Moses to lead them to the Promised Land, a land filled with many good things. The good life they had longed for awaited them, but there was a problem. Pharaoh let them go, but he sent his army after them and the Red Sea blocked their path forward. They were in a situation they could not get out of without divine intervention. The Red Sea was in front of them, and the Egyptian army was behind them. They were ready to return to Egypt because they thought their only other option was to die in the wilderness. Trusting God to intervene on their behalf did not occur to them. Often when we see a situation that appears impossible, we are ready to do what they were going to do—run!

And Moses said to the people, "Do not be afraid. Stand still, and see the salvation of the LORD, which He will accomplish for you today. For the Egyptians whom you see today, you shall see again no more forever. The LORD will fight for you, and you shall hold your peace." And the LORD said to Moses, "Why do you cry to Me? Tell the children of Israel to go forward."

Exodus 14:13–15 NKJV

These verses remind us that our battles belong to the Lord and show us how to let Him fight them for us. First, we cannot run away from problems; we have to stand and face them. And second, we also have to move toward them in faith, trusting God to help us overcome them. "Don't run away, go forward" is a perfect picture of courage.

To go forward when you feel afraid is courage. Courage is not the absence of fear, problems, or seemingly impossible obstacles, but going forward when you feel afraid, believing God will be with you as you keep moving toward your goal.

The problem of running is not a new one. The Bible is filled with stories of people who ran, but interestingly, I have found that God always brought them back to the places they ran from. You see, we conquer nothing by running away. The message of Exodus 14:13–15 is profound and actually gives us the answer to many of life's problems: Don't run, but stand still, stay calm, and then go forward when God leads you, and He will fight for you.

> Don't run, but stand still, stay calm, and then go forward when God leads you, and He will fight for you.

As the Israelites followed the advice God gave them through Moses, He did the impossible. He parted the Red Sea and the people walked through it on dry ground. But when the Egyptian army followed, the sea closed up over them and they all drowned. Nothing is impossible with God! Disobedience never leads us to the miracle-working power of God, but obedience does.

Moses ran from Egypt when someone saw him kill an Egyptian in an effort to help his people, but after forty years in the wilderness God sent him back to Egypt. He had to return to the place he ran from in order to fulfill God's purpose for him (see Acts 7:23–36).

Hagar ran from her mistress, Sarah, and God told her to go back to her and submit to her control (see Gen. 16:8–9). At first glance this could seem very unfair. After all, Sarah mistreated Hagar, but we must not forget that Hagar had a wrong attitude toward Sarah. We frequently see what others do to us as wrong, but we don't see what we may also be doing wrong. We want to run from our discomfort and pain, but God keeps us there until we see our part in the problem and let Him help us correct our behavior. Most of the things we run from are the very tools God has chosen to use to help us mature.

Elijah ran from Jezebel and hid in the wilderness, but when he finally met with God, he was told to get back to work. He could not be God's prophet if he was a coward (see 1 Kings 19:1–16).

Jonah ran from God's call and found himself in a terrible mess. He cried out to God and was delivered, but he had to go back and complete the assignment he had refused to do (see Jonah 1–3).

King David ran from (ignored) his sin of adultery with Bathsheba and the murder of her husband for at least a year. But God sent Nathan the prophet to confront him and to help him face the truth and repent (see 2 Sam. 12:1–9; Ps. 51).

People run from difficulties for all kinds of reasons and in various ways. We may run from responsibility, accountability, hard work, difficult people, challenging places, our sin, ourselves, the truth, the past, and many other things. We may remove ourselves physically from a situation. We may stay too busy to deal with the problem, or we may try to escape it through substance abuse and addictions. But there are two ways we run that I want to discuss in greater detail—making excuses and blaming others.

Excuses Keep Us Trapped

I once heard that an excuse is nothing more than a reason stuffed with a lie. That may sound harsh, but if we are honest we will admit that is exactly what it is. Even if unjust things have happened to us and caused us to behave badly, we must not let them become an excuse to remain that way. Jesus came to set us free from all bondage, but He won't do so while we run and try to hide from the truth. Every excuse we make for bad behavior keeps us trapped in it.

> *Every excuse we make for bad behavior keeps us trapped in it.*

There are many biblical examples of people who made excuses for not obeying God. Jesus tells us a parable about a man who hosted a big dinner party and invited many guests. This represents the invitation God gives everyone—an invitation to believe in Jesus, to be born again, and to receive forgiveness for sins. Let's look at the excuses people gave.

"But they all alike began to make excuses. The first one said to him, 'I have purchased a piece of land and I have to go out and see it; please consider me excused.' Another one said, 'I have purchased five yoke of oxen, and I am going to try them out; please consider me excused.' And

another said, 'I have [recently] married a wife, and for
that reason I am unable to come.'"

Luke 14:18–20

What a great example of the types of excuses many people
make for not putting God first in their lives. They are busy taking care of the things He has provided. We would have nothing
without God's goodness, and then we often repay Him by letting
the things He gives us draw us away from Him.

This parable offers us many different valuable lessons, but we
will look only at the fact that excuses seem to keep many people
from being obedient to God or from doing what they should be
doing.

The apostle Paul had to urge the Galatian believers not to let
their newfound liberty in Christ become an excuse for selfishness (see Gal. 5:13). We see a lot of this in our society today.
People demand their liberties, but are often insensitive and selfish regarding how their supposed liberties affect those around
them. Paul said even though we may be free to do a thing, if it
will offend others we should restrain ourselves out of love (see
1 Cor. 10:31–33). Paul was dealing with Gentile and Jewish believers. The Gentiles had no problem not being circumcised or eating
meat offered to idols, and many Jewish believers didn't, either.
But some of them did; thus, Paul urged those who didn't, not to
be selfish in exercising their liberties.

In most cultures today it is acceptable for women to wear pants
(trousers, slacks) even while ministering, but there are still a few
who would be offended by this type of dress. When I travel in
those cultures, I wear dresses or skirts out of love for them.

If we would take one week and truly listen to ourselves, we
might be appalled at the number of excuses we make for not doing

the right thing. We don't call someone back as we said we would, so we make up an excuse instead of simply saying, "I'm sorry. I definitely should have called you as I said I would." We are late for an appointment and we give an excuse such as "The traffic was really bad," when the truth is that we simply didn't leave early enough to be on time.

Thousands upon thousands of couples divorce, citing incompatibility as an excuse. But the truth is that they didn't want to make the effort to learn how to get along, or they were not willing to compromise and sacrifice in order to make room for the differences in their personality and their spouse's. Any two people can easily find many reasons not to get along, but mature people will do everything they can to make a marriage work before they give up.

Some people go from job to job and never stick with anything long enough to learn a trade or be promoted. To defend this instability, they typically cite a problem with the company, the management, the working conditions, or other employees—never laziness or irresponsibility on their part. They start a new job, and before long they find something they don't like and they quit. They continue to do the same thing repeatedly. Finally it becomes difficult and perhaps impossible for them to even get a job because people with reasonable intelligence can see the problem and know that if they hired this person, they would be hiring a problem.

These people never learn that the devil is putting in their heads ideas about things they should be unhappy with. They are deceived, so they never face the real problem, and the devil gets his way and ruins their lives.

I heard about a woman who was getting married for the seventh time, and she went to her pastor with a prayer request that the man she was about to marry would treat her right so they could stay married. She had never realized that she was the only common denominator in all seven relationships and that there was a strong possibility *she* was the problem.

The only way to prevent the devil from deceiving us is to always be willing to take responsibility for our actions no matter what others are doing. If you are looking for the perfect job or spouse, you are already deceived because the only perfect thing that exists is Jesus, and He wants to help us face and deal with the imperfect aspects of our lives in a loving, peaceful way.

There are times when we should leave a job or even a marriage, but when the same thing happens too often, we are likely to be the problem. To keep running from that fact by using excuses only keeps us miserable and in bondage.

Who Are You Blaming?

Another way we avoid dealing with our problems is to blame them on someone else. I recently heard a person mention something that had gone wrong in his home, and he said it was his wife's fault. I said, "I wonder who people that live alone blame their mistakes on?" We both laughed because we realized that we usually blame someone else for what we should take responsibility for.

For example, if I get upset, I think or say it is because Dave or someone else did something to irritate me. Through blaming, I avoid taking responsibility for my lack of self-control. If I am late, I can usually find someone or something to blame it on instead of taking responsibility for my own poor planning. If Dave has to swerve to avoid hitting another car on the highway, it is always the other driver's fault for pulling out in front of him. It is never his fault (☺).

If we would make the effort to truly pay attention to how many excuses we make and how often we blame others for our poor choices, we would be amazed.

Blaming began in the Garden of Eden, when Adam blamed Eve for giving him the fruit that God had forbidden him to eat, and the blame game has never stopped since (see Gen. 3:12). Adam was, I am sure, quite happy to be the one who was supposed to be the head of his home, but he wasn't doing his job or he would have told Eve no when she gave him the fruit and urged him to eat it, as she had done. Eve always gets the blame for original sin, but I think Adam was just as responsible as she was. They both received punishment and chastisement from the Lord, so obviously they were both responsible. Not only did Adam blame Eve, he also blamed God for giving her to him. After their sin they were hiding from God, and when God confronted them, asking why, Adam said, "The woman whom you gave to be with me, she gave me fruit of the tree, and I ate" (Gen. 3:12 ESV).

There are times when we, like Adam, blame our problems or the injustices done to us on God. Many people are angry with God because of the pain they have experienced, but He is not the source of our problems. The devil is. If we are going to be angry with anyone we should be angry with the devil. The only way to get him back for what he has done to us is to do as much good as we possibly can—the only way to overcome evil is with good (see Rom. 12:21).

During their years in the wilderness, the Israelites blamed Moses and God for their troubles, but the truth is that their problems were due to their own bad attitude (see Num. 21:4–5).

It is time to stop running. Stand still, be silent, and see the salvation of the Lord. He will fight your battles for you, but only if you confront them with Him by your side.

The Journey

Gaining freedom from bondage is a journey. It is a journey back to the things we ran away from and learning that we can do all things through Christ Who is our strength (see Phil. 4:13). As we face our issues, we learn they no longer have power over us. In our walk with God, we are continually learning and changing.

My childhood was filled with violence, incest, and the fear of my father, and my mother would not face and deal with any of it. I saw firsthand the tragic result of running and hiding from problems that needed to be confronted, yet I left home and did the same thing for a number of years. I thought that because I had left home, I had left the problem behind, but I failed to understand that it was etched in my soul and that I needed inner healing.

My soul—thoughts, emotions, and will—were very dysfunctional, but I made excuses and blamed everyone and everything for my dysfunctional and ungodly behavior. I did anything to keep from facing the past because it was so painful. I didn't realize the only way to move beyond it was to face it.

I used my past as an excuse for my bad behavior and my inability to maintain healthy relationships. But as long as I made excuses, I wasn't facing the past and dealing with it in a godly way. I used the painful, unjust things that had happened to me as reasons not to take responsibility for my improper attitudes and actions. When you reach the end of this chapter, it might be a good time to take a break from reading and ask yourself if you are doing the same thing in any area of your life. Remember, although the truth hurts, it is the one thing that makes us free (see John 8:32).

Deliverance comes when we learn to stand still (stop running) and confront the problems we prefer to avoid. Is there anything you are running from? If so, open your heart to God in that area and ask Him to do whatever He needs to do in order to set you free from it. As He does, take steps of obedience and be assured that each one will take you a little closer to enjoying the life Jesus desires for you. Then you will see the salvation of the Lord, and see God fight your battles.

When we stand still and face difficulties, thankfully we don't have to do it alone. We are God's children, and He will guide us, restore us, heal us, and be with us every step of the way. If you need healing in your soul, I recommend my book *Healing the Soul of a Woman*, which takes you through the journey from brokenness to wholeness. I believe it will help you move forward.

When I say we need to face the past, I mean we need to fully accept either what we have done wrong or what others have done to us. We need to realize that although we cannot go back and undo what has happened, we can be set free and even be made stronger because of it. God can take the worst things in our lives and make them our greatest blessings. Remember, nothing is impossible with Him (see Luke 1:37).

> God can take the worst things in our lives and make them our greatest blessings.

CHAPTER 15

Spiritual Warfare God's Way, Part 1

"Not by might, nor by power, but by my Spirit, says the
Lord of hosts."

Zechariah 4:6 ESV

Understanding or helping others understand how to fight against an invisible enemy with invisible weapons while wearing invisible armor is very challenging. The enemy, the weapons, and the armor are all undeniably real in the spiritual realm, but that realm cannot be seen with the natural eye unless, of course, God miraculously opens a person's eyes and allows a glimpse into it.

Although we cannot see the devil, we can easily learn to discern and recognize the fruit of his activity. Strife, hatred, anger, war, famine, disease, disasters, tragedy, insecurity, addictions, and thousands of other things are the works of the devil. Jesus said that the thief, meaning the devil, "comes only in order to steal and kill and destroy" (John 10:10). In the same verse, Jesus also said that He came to give us life and to give it "in abundance [to the full, till it overflows]." The Greek word translated *life* in this verse means "life as God has it"—that is, the type and quality of life God offers. Jesus didn't come to Earth so we could walk around and be miserable, but so we could overcome all the works of the enemy and enjoy life as God intends for us to enjoy it.

Jesus didn't come simply to give us the promise of heaven

when we die, but to give us a life worth living while we are on our way to Heaven. Eternal life doesn't begin when we die; it starts the moment we are born again. Jesus came to give us victory and make us more than conquerors (see Rom. 8:37). He also came to destroy the works of the evil one (see 1 John 3:8), which does not mean to make them disappear, but to give us the strength to overcome them through our faith in Him.

Waging spiritual warfare successfully requires thoughtful planning and strategies. In this chapter and the next one, I will explain those strategies and offer you a plan that will help you every time you are in a battle with the enemy.

> *Waging spiritual warfare successfully requires thoughtful planning and strategies.*

Strategy #1: Worship

First, let me say that the strategies we use to fight the spiritual war are not the ways the world fights. Actually, they are the opposite of anything we would think fighting might be. If you remember the strategy God gave Jehoshaphat to fight his battle, you will recall that nothing he did should have defeated the enemy. But since he acted in obedience to God and did what would seem foolish to the world, God fought for him and defeated his enemy. Through his obedience he let God fight his battle.

Jehoshaphat worshipped God and sent singers to sing, and God defeated his enemy. So we see that worship wins the war, and *worship* is defined as "reverence and adoration of a deity." According to biblical examples, worship may also involve physically bowing on our knees and even bowing low and placing our faces on the ground. Jehoshaphat bowed with his face to the ground and worshipped (see 2 Chron. 20:18). Today we think we are worshipping if we sing a song in church, but the true meaning of the word *worship* certainly involves more than that.

How could a person fight a war while bowing on his knees? That would seem to give the enemy an advantage and the freedom to attack. But when we bow in reverence and true worship, we put ourselves in a position in which we are very vulnerable unless God comes through and fights for us. This was a position of total trust on Jehoshaphat's part. He must have realized a powerful enemy was close to attacking and possibly annihilating him and his people— and his only defense was to bow in worship and send singers to sing. I am not indicating that we *must* bow on our knees in order to worship God, but it is an example of worship in Scripture.

God has given the church many songs that move us in spirit, and just as singers were part of God's battle plan for Jehoshaphat and his people, when we sing to and about the Lord, we wage a specific kind of warfare that is understood only in the spiritual realm. Many of us can testify that God has used a specific song to strengthen and minister to us in difficult times.

Another example of the power of worship in warfare is when Paul and Silas sang and prayed at midnight while they were in prison, and suddenly the prison doors opened supernaturally (see Acts 16:25–26).

Satan hates Spirit-filled music. Some Bible translators believe Satan was once a worship leader in heaven, based on the King James Version of Ezekiel 28:13. Whether he was or not, it is evident that he hates godly music and that music can be very effective in spiritual warfare. The ability to sing is a gift from God, and even if all we can do is make a joyful noise, it is enough to help us in our battles.

Strategy #2: Rest

When I began to learn who my true enemy was, understanding that I had authority and power over him and knowing I could and should do warfare against him, I found it exhausting. I seemed to be fighting against or resisting something almost all the time. But the really frustrating part of it was that no matter what I did, it didn't help.

One of my problems was that I was trying to get my difficulties to disappear, but God's goal was to make me strong enough that those problems didn't bother me. One day I sensed the Lord speaking this question in my heart: "Joyce, how did Jesus wage spiritual warfare?" As I thought about it and compared what I was doing to the way Jesus dealt with the devil, I quickly recognized that what He did was very different from what I was doing.

> How did Jesus wage spiritual warfare?

The devil has probably never attacked anyone as often and as intently as he did Jesus, yet we never see Jesus lose control or even seem worried, afraid, or upset by anything the enemy did. Why? Part of the answer is that He knew Who He was and where He came from. He also knew what He was sent to do and where He was going after His job was complete. We can and should know these same things. You and I are children of God; we came from Him and are created in His image; He has a plan for our lives, and when our time here on Earth is over, we will go to Heaven and dwell in His presence forever (see Rom. 8:16, 29; Acts 2:28). This knowledge should give us a fresh perspective on fighting the devil simply because no matter what he does, we have already won the battle. Our destiny is settled. Our home is waiting for us in Heaven, where we will live with God for eternity.

When Jesus was raised from the dead, Satan's fate was settled, and we are merely walking out our part of God's overall plan until the final enemy—death—is defeated.

As I began seriously looking at Jesus' response to Satan's attacks, I realized that one thing He did was to enter God's rest. The rest God offers is referred to as a "Sabbath rest" (see Heb. 4:9–10), and it involves much more than setting aside one day of the week not to work. The Sabbath the Old Testament Jews observed was a type and shadow of the true Sabbath rest God offers us now.

Vine's Greek New Testament Dictionary says the kind of rest God offers "is not a 'rest' *from* work but *in* work" (italics mine) (gospelhall.org/bible). It is not inactivity, but resting while being active. It is the harmonious working together of all your faculties because each has found its sphere of satisfaction in Christ. When we are enjoying the rest of God, we are not worried, emotionally upset, or willfully trying to take care of problems ourselves without leaning on God. We are not relentlessly trying to figure out what we should do; we are telling God that we don't know what to do, but our trust is in Him.

This helps us understand Paul's statement in Ephesians 6:13 regarding spiritual warfare, to do all the crisis demands and to stand firmly in our place. We can do what God asks us to do, but do it from a position of rest rather than one of worry, reasoning, fear, frustration, and struggle.

Hebrews 4:10 teaches us to cease "from [the weariness and pain of] . . . [human] labors" and enter into the rest of God. When Jesus ascended to Heaven after His resurrection, He was told to come and sit at God's right hand (signifying rest) until His enemies were made a stool for His feet (see Acts 2:32–35). This statement makes it clear that God the Father has further plans for Satan's total defeat. Jesus had done His part; now He was to simply enter God's supernatural rest and wait until God finished what only He could do.

This is a perfect picture of what we are also supposed to do, which is to do what God tells us to do, or whatever we can do in the crisis at hand, and then enter God's rest and wait for Him to do what only He can do.

Jesus is always depicted as seated in heavenly places, not standing but seated (see Eph. 1:20; Heb. 8:1). This implies rest, and it was not available until Jesus died for our sins, descended into Hell, took the keys of Hell and death away from Satan, and rose victoriously. Satan is already defeated, and by entering God's rest when we face crises in our lives, we show that we trust and believe that God will take care of us. The enemy can come against us, but he cannot defeat us if we walk in the truth that our battles belong to the Lord and we learn to let Him fight them for us.

Strategy #3: Remain Calm in Adversity

God wants us to stay calm in adversity, and according to Psalm 94:12–13, He disciplines us by trial until we learn to do so. In other words, we go through difficulties until we learn not to let them frighten or disturb us. Our difficulties do not come from God, but He does use them to help us grow spiritually.

Let's look at Paul's attitude during times of great trial:

> We are afflicted in every way, but not crushed; perplexed, but not driven to despair; persecuted, but not forsaken; struck down, but not destroyed; always carrying in the body the death of Jesus, so that the life of Jesus may also be manifested in our bodies.
>
> 2 Corinthians 4:8–10 ESV

So we do not lose heart. Though our outer self is wasting away, our inner self is being renewed day by day. For this light momentary affliction is preparing for us an eternal weight of glory beyond all comparison, as we look not to the things that are seen but to the things that are unseen. For the things that are seen are transient, but the things that are unseen are eternal.

2 Corinthians 4:16–18 ESV

Paul did not state that his trials were easy, but he did say that they did not make him worry, fear, become anxious, or despair. He endured difficulties, but he remained in God's rest. Going through a trial is enough to deal with on its own without having to worry and be anxious about it. Thank God for His gracious invitation to enter His rest!

Rest is warfare in the spiritual realm simply because Satan cannot understand how we can have such intense problems and rest in the midst of them. Jehoshaphat was delivered while worshipping and singing, and entering the rest of God does the same for us. We rest, God works, and we enjoy the benefit.

Strategy #4: Stay Protected by God's Presence

Understanding the importance of dwelling in God's presence is the next important subject I want to talk about in this chapter. I spent too many years seeking His presents (what He could do for me) when I should have been seeking His presence (Who He is). Recognizing the value and power of God's presence whether He is doing anything for us or not at that moment is very important. It is Him we need, not what He can do for us. We need to learn to seek God's face, not just His hand.

> *Anything besides God that we feel we have to have to be satisfied is something the devil can use against us.*

Anything besides God that we feel we have to have to be satisfied is something the devil can use against us. We all want many things, but only one thing is needful, and that is God Himself.

When God sent Moses to take the people into the Promised Land, Moses said to Him, "See, you say to me, 'Bring up this people,' but you have not let me know whom you will send with me. Yet you have said, 'I know you by name, and you have also found favor in my sight.' Now therefore, if I have found favor in your sight, please show me now your ways, that I may know you in order to find favor in your sight. Consider too that this nation is your people" (Exod. 33:12–13 ESV).

Notice that Moses requested God do something to prove His favor toward him. But God said, "My presence will go with you, and I will give you rest" (Exod. 33:14 ESV). Moses quickly responded, "If your presence will not go with me, do not bring us up from here" (Exod. 33:15 ESV).

Moses was wise enough to know that if God's presence was not with him, there was no purpose in going because he would surely be defeated. God's presence is always with us because He promised to never leave or forsake us (see Deut. 31:6).

Brother Lawrence, a monk who lived during the 1600s, decided to dedicate his life to practicing the presence of God and to never go very long without being consciously aware that God was with him. It took many years to fully form the habit of doing so, but at least he realized the importance of seeking God more than anything else. You and I need to recognize the importance of seeking His presence, just as Brother Lawrence did.

How long do you go without even thinking about God? Jeremiah said that God's people went days without number and never even thought about Him (see Jer. 2:32). We should not think of God only on Sunday mornings when we go to church or merely when we have a problem with which we need His help. He wants and deserves to be involved in all we do. We need His presence all the time, and He is never more than one thought away.

In Joshua 6:8–9, when the Israelites marched into battle, the seven priests carrying the seven trumpets and the ark of the covenant, which carried the presence of God, led the way. They knew God had to go first or they would be slaughtered.

The psalmist David has a great deal to say about the importance of the presence of God:

- In Psalm 27:4–6 he writes that there is only one thing he desires: to behold God's beauty and dwell in His presence all the days of his life.
- He says that God will hide him in His shelter in the day of trouble and that his head would be lifted above his enemies (see Ps. 27:5–6). We can see from this that dwelling in God's presence is a form of spiritual warfare. When we seek God, He protects us from our enemies.
- In Psalm 31:20, David writes that we are hidden "from the strife of tongues" in the presence of God. As a public figure I am aware that some people may say unkind things about me, and this Scripture gives me comfort. It is great to know that in God's presence, I am hidden from the strife-filled comments people may make about me.
- Psalm 91:1 declares that the one who dwells in the shelter of the Most High will abide in the shadow of the Almighty, and the remainder of the Psalm is about how that person will be protected and delivered. Verses 9–10 say that if we

make the Lord our dwelling place, no evil will be allowed to befall us.

I love all these marvelous promises of protection for those who seek God's presence. If you make seeking God a priority, you will be doing spiritual warfare, perhaps without even realizing it.

Here are a few suggestions for how you can practice making God's presence more of a priority in your life:

- Practice seeking God for Who He is, not just for what He can do for you. You might even take a few days to avoid asking God for anything other than Himself.
- Start each day spending time with God in His Word or simply talking with Him. Tell Him you have no desire to do anything without Him, and ask Him to make His presence real to you.
- Stop what you're doing several times a day and remind yourself that God is with you right now! Tell God you need Him and appreciate His presence in your life.
- Thank God throughout the day. There are hundreds of things we can thank Him for daily if we make a habit of doing so.

Learning to practice God's presence will require forming some habits that will help you do it, and that takes time. Don't be impatient with yourself if you get busy and find you've gone through the day without thinking about Him. Just tell Him you are sorry and celebrate the times you do remember. God appreciates any effort we make to seek Him or to know Him better.

We are protected in and by God's presence! Spending time with God, whether for a few hours or even a few minutes, is a type of spiritual warfare, and it is very enjoyable.

CHAPTER 16

Spiritual Warfare God's Way, Part 2

Submit yourselves therefore to God. Resist the devil, and he will flee from you.

James 4:7 ESV

The only way to gain victory over the enemy in a spiritual war is to follow God's directions, not to do it in ways we might think would be effective. In this chapter, I want to share with you four more strategies for winning the spiritual war by fighting it God's way.

Strategy #5: Obedience

We often hear people quote only the last half of James 4:7. They say, "Resist the devil, and he will flee from you" (ESV), but that is not the entire verse. Focusing on only half of the verse is dangerous because there is no way to resist the devil unless we first submit to God and His will.

Actually, anytime we submit to God and do what He asks instead of doing what we may want to do, we engage in spiritual warfare. Satan hates it when we obey God, and our obedience is a powerful force against him.

One is to simply be obedient to God! All disobedience opens a door for the enemy and gives him access to our lives. This is especially the case if we are aware that what we are doing is against God's will and do it anyway.

Let's remember Jesus in the Garden of Gethsemane when He asked for His suffering to pass if possible. But He quickly added, "Not my will, but yours, be done" (Luke 22:42 ESV). We can ask for anything we want, but should always be clear that if what we want is not God's will, we don't want it. When I pray, I frequently say after making a request, "Lord, if what I am asking isn't Your will, please don't give it to me."

> "Lord, if what I am asking isn't Your will, please don't give it to me."

A good place to begin walking in greater obedience in our lives is to take our thoughts captive to the obedience of Christ (see 2 Cor. 10:5). Our thoughts are private, and no one knows what they are except God and us, so we strike a blow to the enemy when we honor God by bringing our thoughts into obedience to Him and to His Word. More than anything else, the enemy wants to control the way we think because the way we think will become the way we behave.

Obedience to God is how we show our love for Him. Jesus said, "If you love me, you will keep my commandments" (John 14:15 ESV). I want to point out that He did not say, "If you obey Me, I will love you." God already loves us unconditionally. His love for us is not based on our obedience, but obedience is the way we demonstrate our love for Him. The apostle John writes, "This is love, that we walk according to His commandments. This is the commandment, that as you have heard from the beginning, you should walk in it" (2 John 1:6 NKJV). And Jesus says that we are blessed when we hear the word of God and obey it (see Luke 11:28).

Strategy #6: Use the Power of Words

Another way we can and should do spiritual warfare is through the words we speak. The Bible is filled with insight and wisdom about the importance of words. I never write a book without at least including some teaching on the power of words. We can wage warfare with our words.

One of the best examples of this is in Luke 4:1–12. The Holy Spirit led Jesus into the wilderness for forty days and the devil tempted Him there. When He was hungry Satan suggested that if He was the Son of God, He could use His power and turn the stones around Him into bread. Jesus said to the devil, "It is written, 'Man shall not live by bread alone'" (Luke 4:4 ESV). Satan did not give up; he showed Jesus "all the kingdoms of the world in a moment of time, and said to him, 'To you I will give all this authority and their glory, for it has been delivered to me, and I give it to whom I will. If you, then, will worship me, it will all be yours.' And Jesus answered him, 'It is written, "You shall worship the Lord your God, and him only shall you serve"'" (Luke 4:5-8 ESV).

Satan said the kingdoms of the world had been given to him, but God certainly wasn't the one who gave them to him. So who did? Adam and Eve gave them to him. When they disobeyed God and listened to Satan's lies, they allowed him to steal the authority God had given them. Jesus came and took that authority back from the devil and has now given it back to us, but we have to believe in it and walk in it, or it does us no good. Just as Adam and Eve gave up their authority through disobedience, we take back our authority and maintain it through being obedient to God.

When Satan talked to Jesus, Jesus talked back to him, and we need to do the same. Jesus used God's Word and answered Satan's temptations with Scripture. Satan doesn't give up easily. Verses 9–11 say: "And he took Jesus to Jerusalem and set him on the pinnacle of the temple and said to him, 'If you are the Son of God, throw yourself down from here, for it is written, "He will command his angels concerning you, to guard you," and "On their hands they will bear you up, lest you strike your foot against a stone"'" (ESV). You will notice that Satan knows Scripture, and he will even try to use it in improper ways to draw us into disobedience. But since Jesus knew the truth He answered Satan, "It is said, 'You shall not put the Lord your God to the test'" (Luke 4:12 ESV). The story concludes with these words: "And when the devil had ended every temptation, he departed from him until an opportune time" (Luke 4:13 ESV).

We can learn so much about doing warfare God's way by studying this section of Scripture. Jesus fought the devil with the Word of God. He talked back to the devil, and we can and should do likewise. Jeremiah prophesied, "Let him who has my word speak my word faithfully" (Jer. 23:28 ESV).

> *When Satan lies to you, do you recognize his lies and talk back to him?*

When Satan lies to you, do you recognize his lies and talk back to him? If not, you need to begin to do so. When thoughts you don't want come into your head, the best way to get rid of them is to speak aloud something you do want to think about.

Remember, one piece of our armor is the sword of the Spirit, which is the Word of God. Paul said the Word of God is sharp like a sword (see Heb. 4:12), but it does us no good unless we use it, and we do that by studying, meditating on, and speaking God's Word. God's Word contains truth to defeat every lie of Satan, and if we know that truth we can use it against him. The purpose of studying God's Word is to meditate on it and let it renew our minds, teach us to think properly, and enable us to recognize the lies of the enemy. It is also so we can speak the Word and wage spiritual warfare with it.

Notice that two of the temptations Satan launched against Jesus concerned His identity as the Son of God. I believe identity is also an area about which Satan lies to us. He accuses us, hoping to make us feel worthless and guilty. He tries to make us feel insignificant and unloved, and he wants us to believe that God is not pleased with us. This is why I try so hard to teach people who they are in Christ and that God loves them unconditionally. It is so important for them to know they are gifted, valuable, and part of God's plan. It is vital for them to know He adores them and will never leave or forsake them.

For many Christians, the thought of talking back to the devil, or speaking out loud against the lies of the devil, may seem foolish, but we can see that Jesus did it. If He did it, we should do it, too.

However, there is a time for everything (see Eccles. 3:1). There is a time to talk and a time to be quiet. We need to know not only when to talk and what to say, but when to say nothing at all. The power of life and death is in the tongue (see Prov. 18:21).

People who are emotionally distraught are usually tempted to talk about how they feel, and that can be dangerous. If we cannot say something positive during trials, we should choose to just be quiet. Jesus once told His disciples He would not be speaking with them much more because the evil ruler of the world was coming. He stated that the devil had no claim on Him, meaning that there was nothing in Him that belonged to the powers of darkness (see John 14:30). Evidently He was determined not to say anything that could give Satan an open door, so He intentionally stayed quiet.

A similar Scripture, a prophecy about Jesus, is Isaiah 53:7: "He was oppressed, [yet when] He was afflicted, He was submissive and opened not His mouth; like a lamb that is led to the slaughter, and as a sheep before her shearers is dumb, so He opened not His mouth" (AMPC).

We are often tempted to say things that should not be said, and I recommend that we pray about this regularly. Jesus said, "Pray that you may not fall into temptation" (Luke 22:46). I rarely miss a day without asking God to put a guard over my mouth so I don't sin with my tongue (see Ps. 141:3). No one can tame the tongue without help from God. James said it is a restless evil full of deadly poison (see James 3:8). Wow! I think that sounds serious enough to warrant regular prayer, don't you?

As I leave the subject of doing warfare with words, let me quote one of the Bible's most powerful Scriptures about the words we speak.

> Let no foul or polluting language, nor evil word nor unwholesome or worthless talk [ever] come out of your mouth, but only such [speech] as is good and beneficial to the spiritual progress of others, as is fitting to the need and the occasion, that it may be a blessing and give grace (God's favor) to those who hear it.
>
> Ephesians 4:29 AMPC

Strategy #7: Love

Learning that walking in love is spiritual warfare was very exciting to me, and it has benefited my life in many ways. As we study the Bible, although it teaches us many things, there are a few subjects we might say stand out as things we don't want to miss or take lightly. The subject of love is one of them.

When asked what was the greatest and most important commandment, Jesus said, " 'You shall love the Lord your God with all your heart, and with all your soul, and with all your mind.' This is the first and greatest commandment. The second is like it, 'You shall love your neighbor as yourself' " (Matt. 22:37–39).

In 1 Corinthians 13:2–3, Paul teaches that no matter what we do or how much faith we have—even if we give away everything we have and sacrifice our lives—if we don't have love we gain nothing. He also teaches that faith works by and is energized by love (see Gal. 5:6). So no matter how much we try to exercise our faith, if we are not walking in love, our faith is powerless. Paul also wrote to Timothy, a young minister, that the aim of his calling and charge from God was love that comes "from a pure heart and a good conscience and a sincere faith" (1 Tim. 1:5). These Scriptures all make essentially the same point: Love is the greatest, most important thing in the world.

God loves us, and it is His love that sent Jesus to save us. It is His love that heals us, and it is His love flowing through us to others that should be our goal. Satan tempts us with things that are the opposite of love because when we walk in genuine love, it provides a strong defense against him. For example, if you are angry with someone, and you choose to forgive that person and cover the offense with love right now, you would be waging spiritual warfare.

Everyone on the planet is searching for love. We want to be loved! Love has the power to accomplish many wonderful things. It heals broken hearts, gives hope to the hopeless, helps provide for the poor and needy, and edifies and encourages the discouraged and depressed. Loving people makes them feel valuable.

Love is not merely a word or a topic for a Sunday morning sermon; it is a power that can be seen and felt. Love takes action, and it has to flow in order to stay alive. We are never happier than when we are showing love to others. Most of us make the mistake of thinking happiness comes by getting everything we want, but that makes us selfish and miserable. Although it sounds like it couldn't work, the truth is that doing things for others and giving to others is the source of true joy.

We recently met a financial need for a friend of ours, and although my flesh didn't particularly want to let go of the money, I knew God wanted us to give it. By obeying God and showing love, we were doing spiritual warfare. Reaching out in love is like building walls of protection around oneself.

Strategy #8: Overcome Evil with Good

As I have mentioned several times in this book, Romans 12:21 says that we overcome evil with good; therefore, I say that we defeat the devil (wage spiritual warfare) by being good to and loving others. This is especially powerful when we are under attack from the enemy, going through circumstances that

> We defeat the devil (wage spiritual warfare) by being good to and loving others.

are difficult and painful. Instead of turning inward and thinking about how miserable we are and how unjustly we are being treated, we should purpose to pray about what we need God to help us with and then cast our care on Him and stay busy blessing others.

When Satan attacks he expects to make us miserable and self-centered, but if we respond to his attacks with acts of kindness and meeting the needs of others, he becomes confused and then defeated. If we tend to God's business, which is loving people, then He will take care of ours. He will fight our battles and make sure we win.

Loving others, especially when we are hurting, is something we will never "feel" like doing, so we must do it on purpose. We must discipline ourselves to love, and although this type of discipline seems painful rather than pleasant, later on it yields good fruit (see Heb. 12:11).

The Danger of Anger

A large part of loving others involves letting go of anger when people hurt or disappoint us, and the way we do that is by forgiving them. We must be quick to forgive and always remember that God has forgiven us for far more than we will ever be required to forgive others.

Many Christians live angry lives and pay little attention to the Bible's repeated teachings about the danger of anger and unforgiveness. Paul writes that we should not let our anger lead us into sin, nor should we let the sun go down on our anger. If we do, we give the devil an opportunity to work in our lives (see Eph. 4:26–27). God doesn't expect us never to feel the emotion of anger, but He does expect us not to allow it to lead us into sin. We can feel wrong and still choose to do right.

Paul writes in 2 Corinthians 2:10–11 that it is important to forgive in order to keep Satan from gaining an advantage over us and not to be ignorant of his schemes. Trying to keep us angry, bitter, resentful, and unforgiving is one of Satan's most vicious strategies, and if we do not resist him in these areas, it will do untold damage to our lives.

Jesus teaches that if we do not forgive others when they trespass against us, God will not forgive our trespasses (see Matt.

6:15). I wonder how many people don't understand why they can't seem to feel close to the Lord or why their prayers are not answered, yet they harbor anger and refuse to forgive those who have wronged them.

I pray that you will take these thoughts seriously. There is no point in expecting God to fight our battles for us if we won't obey Him by forgiving those who have hurt us.

Why Is It So Hard to Forgive?

Forgiving others can be very difficult unless we do it God's way. He has told us to pray for our enemies and to bless, not curse, them. Luke even writes that we should be kind to them.

> "But I say to you who hear, Love your enemies, do good to those who hate you, bless those who curse you, pray for those who abuse you."
>
> Luke 6:27–28 ESV

We make the decision to obey God by doing what these Scriptures say to do. Then God will heal our wounded emotions and vindicate us. We can obey God's Word if we don't let our feelings rule over us. It may not seem fair, but God is a God of justice, and He makes wrong things right if we do as He instructs. We don't have to fight with people. God will fight our battles for us if we fight with love rather than hatred.

I strongly encourage you to decide right now that with God's help, you will not waste another day of your life being angry. Start fighting with love and forgiveness, and you will easily defeat the devil.

CHAPTER 17

The Power of a Thankful Life

*When he had taken counsel with the people, he appointed those who were to sing to the L*ORD *and praise him in holy attire, as they went before the army, and say, "Give thanks to the L*ORD, *for his steadfast love endures forever."*

2 Chronicles 20:21 ESV

Remember that Jehoshaphat won his battle by following the Lord's instructions. He was told that he would not need to fight in the battle he faced, and to hold his position and see the salvation of the Lord. He bowed before God, worshipped Him, and sent singers out to sing. It's interesting that the singers were to sing something very specific: "Give thanks to the LORD, for his steadfast love endures forever" (2 Chron. 20:21 ESV). When they began to sing, the Lord defeated their enemies.

The power of praise and worship is amazing, as is the giving of thanks. We are to "be thankful and say so to Him" (Ps. 100:4 AMPC). Apparently voicing thankfulness is important. Try taking one whole day each week to thank God for things like clean water, a warm home in the winter, food to eat, friends and family to love, and thousands of other things we can easily take for granted unless we purpose to recognize and be thankful for them.

If we keep our minds and mouths full of thanksgiving, we will do a lot less complaining. We have all heard "Count your blessings," but what if we actually did it? Counting our blessings, or thinking about them regularly, is one way to never start taking them for granted nor to develop an attitude of entitlement. How long has it been since you thanked God for clean water, or for living in a home with heat and air-conditioning? Millions of people around the world have none of those conveniences, and they find other things to thank God for. We all have much for which to be thankful, but it is possible to be so focused on what we don't have or what we need that we fail to see what we do have, let alone be thankful for it.

Complaining Does Not Defeat the Devil

There is no complaint department in Heaven! God doesn't answer complaints. He only answers prayers and petitions offered with thanksgiving (see Phil. 4:6). Why should God give us more of anything if we are unhappy with what we already have and complaining about it? It is not what we have or don't have that makes us grumpy or thankful, it is our attitude. It is an issue of character. There are hundreds of Scriptures that use the word *thanksgiving*, some form of it, or words related to it (such as *gratitude*) in the Bible. Anything repeated so often in God's Word must surely be important. I have a feeling that merely being more thankful and focusing on our blessings would change a lot of things in our lives for the better. It would also disable the enemy and deny him access to us.

> Why should God give us more of anything if we are unhappy with what we already have and complaining about it?

I have to go to a wedding tonight. It is a long way away from my home, and I have found myself murmuring in my heart to the Lord about how far away it is and how late I will get home. But the good news is that I got invited! I have something to do tonight while multitudes of people will sit home alone, people who would be delighted to have the invitation I received. I am sure we can all think of many situations like this in our lives, but we can be thankful on purpose. Our joy increases dramatically if we simply change our perspective and look for the things for which we can be thankful rather than complain about the inconveniences and challenges we encounter.

Complaining does not defeat the devil, but it does open a door of opportunity for him to harass us. The Israelites spent forty years in the wilderness on a journey that should have taken eleven days (see Deut. 1:2). They wandered around and around the same mountains, doing the same things over and over again. The Promised Land was in front of them, but they could not get there without defeating the enemies that stood between them and the land God had promised them. Instead of asking God for direction and being obedient to Him, they did a lot of complaining.

In 1 Corinthians 10:1–10, Paul writes about the Israelites' plight, encouraging us not to make the same mistakes they did. He urges us to let what happened to the Israelites be an example to us so we can avoid the same behavior.

He told them not to indulge in immorality as some of the Israelites did, after which twenty-three thousand of them fell dead in a single day. He said we are not to put Christ to the test, as some of them did and were destroyed by serpents (representing the devil), nor should we murmur as some of them did and were destroyed by the destroyer (see 1 Cor. 10: 8–10).

I strongly encourage you to read these verses again and take them seriously. Complaining opens a door for the devil to bring destruction into our lives, but other Scriptures clearly show that thankfulness keeps doors tightly closed when he tries to enter. Complaining adds to our misery while thankfulness releases joy.

Meister Eckhart said, "If the only prayer you ever say in your entire life is thank you, it will be enough." One man said that he once complained about having no shoes until he met a man who had no feet.

I doubt that any of us can even imagine how powerful our lives would be if we lived daily with hearts filled with gratitude. But even if we have made mistakes in the past by complaining too much and not being thankful enough, we can have a new beginning and it can start today.

Are You Willing to Take Action?

Don't ever complain about something you are not willing to do anything about. As an example, you might complain about not getting enough sleep, but you could arrange your life in such a way that you do sleep enough. God can't give you more sleep if you won't go to bed at the time that is right for you. Or perhaps you complain frequently about how busy you are, but you keep saying yes to more and more things when you should be cutting some commitments out of your schedule. Or maybe you complain about debt, but you have forgotten that you are the one who spent the money. Perhaps you complain about how bad you feel physically, but you keep eating junk food and never exercise. I once felt tired most of the time and I prayed diligently for God to give me more energy. Instead, He led me to start walking a few miles daily. I did it and started to feel better. Sometimes we look for a miracle when all we need is common sense. There are many things we ask God to do for us and we don't get answers, because we are not doing what He has already shown us to do.

> *Sometimes we look for a miracle when all we need is common sense.*

Be content with what you have while you're on your way to getting what you want. Hopefully you have a vision or a dream for your life, and I urge you to enjoy the journey while waiting to see it fulfilled. Each phase or season of life is necessary and valuable, so let your journey be one of gratitude rather than murmuring, grumbling, and complaining. Complaining doesn't speed up your progress, but it will slow it down.

James writes that we are not to complain about one another and bring judgment on ourselves (see James 5:9). Talking about the faults and weaknesses of the people in our lives may be one of our more frequent complaints, but we all have faults. Taking an honest inventory of our own faults helps us cover the offenses of others in a spirit of love. 1 Peter 4:8 says, "Love covers a multitude of sins" (ESV).

I try to thank God daily for my family and friends and to think about all the people in the world who are lonely and have no one with whom to even eat a meal. No person is perfect, and the more you get to know people, the more you may see or notice qualities about them you may not enjoy, but you also see advantages that make the relationship with them valuable. For example, my husband is not a gift buyer, so I rarely get flowers from him unless his secretary sends them for him on Valentine's Day. He seldom just shows up with a gift, and for many years I complained about it. But he does do all kinds of acts of service for me. He does the dishes at night, takes out the trash, and runs errands if I need him to. He is affectionate and never misses a day telling me he loves me. He gives me a lot of freedom to do what I want to do. So I can complain about the things he doesn't do, or I can be thankful for what he does do. Nobody does it all! There simply are no perfect people.

We should not go to God with a complaint without a vision. Habakkuk went to God with a complaint and He said, "Write the vision; make it plain on tablets, so he may run who reads it" (Hab. 2:2 ESV).

Nehemiah heard a complaint about the broken-down walls in Jerusalem (see Neh. 1:3), so he got a vision and a plan to fix them (see Neh. 2:4–18).

If you have a complaint about your job, then start looking for a better one, but stay sweet and thankful at the one you currently have. Many people who cannot find a job at all would probably love to have the one you complain about.

We cannot complain ourselves into a better position in life. We should pray, be thankful for what we do have, and ask God to show us what He wants us to do to make our situation better.

Be a Bright Star

Scripture encourages us to be bright stars shining for God in a dark world.

> Do everything without murmuring or questioning [the providence of God], so that you may prove yourselves to be blameless and guileless, innocent and uncontaminated, children of God without blemish in the midst of a [morally] crooked and [spiritually] perverted generation, among whom you are seen as bright lights [beacons shining out clearly] in the world [of darkness].
>
> Philippians 2:14–15

The Amplified Bible Classic Edition says we are to "do all things without grumbling and faultfinding and complaining." This makes God's will for us very clear. When we are out in the world day after day, we hear more complaining than anything else. Just start to pay attention, and I think you will agree. People complain about the weather, their job, the government, the people in their lives, high prices, and their aches and pains. The list is endless, but God offers us an opportunity to shine brightly for Him by simply refusing to complain. And along with avoiding complaining, we can go a step further and say as many positive things as possible.

Don't Quench the Holy Spirit

Quench means "to stop from working, to extinguish, to snuff out, or to smother." The freedom of the Holy Spirit to work in our lives is vital, so doing anything that quenches or grieves Him is not good.

> In every situation [no matter what the circumstance] be thankful and continually give thanks to God; for this is the will of God for you in Christ Jesus. Do not quench [subdue, or be unresponsive to the working and guidance of] the [Holy] Spirit.
>
> 1 Thessalonians 5:18–19

When I studied these Scriptures many years ago, I began to realize that complaining is a more serious problem than I ever imagined. I doubt I ever get through an entire day without complaining or murmuring about something. I pray I will continue to grow in this area and hopefully someday be able to say I never complain about anything, but I realize that will take a lot of help from God.

> *Can you make it through interruptions and inconvenience without complaining?*

Can you make it through interruptions and inconvenience without complaining? Can you face unexpected difficulties and not complain or murmur? Complaining is a reactionary response to something we don't like. Not complaining is something we have to do on purpose. It requires a lot of discipline and self-control. I also think it requires having the awareness of how dangerous complaining is. Not one of us would want to open a door for the devil and invite him into our lives, and one way we can tightly shut the door to him is to be thankful at all times in all things. Being thankful is the polar opposite of complaining, and it accomplishes a lot for us in the spiritual realm. For example, thanksgiving protects us, strengthens us, and increases our faith. Let's look at each of these benefits in a more detailed way.

Thanksgiving protects us.

Being thankful protects us from self-pity, greed, discouragement, and even depression. I have wasted many days wallowing in these negative emotions because things didn't go my way, but I pray I won't ever waste another day doing that.

Thanksgiving also protects us from our enemies. Deuteronomy 28:47–48 says, "Because you did not serve the Lord your God with joyfulness of [mind and] heart [in gratitude] for the abundance of all [with which He had blessed you], therefore you shall serve your enemies" (AMPC).

Wow! That is an eye-opening Scripture. Because the people were not grateful, they served their enemies. It is obvious from these verses and others that a thankful life is a powerful life.

Thanksgiving strengthens us.

Having a positive, happy, grateful attitude adds strength to our lives, but being negative and complaining drains strength from us. I have heard that it takes fewer muscles to smile than to frown. Likewise being positive gives us strength, while being negative steals strength. Do you want more strength or less?

Paul prayed this for the church at Colossae and I believe for us as well.

> Being strengthened with all power, according to his glorious might, for all endurance and patience with joy; giving thanks to the Father, who has qualified you to share in the inheritance of the saints in light.
>
> Colossians 1:11–12 ESV

In studying Paul's prayers for the various churches he ministered to, I have found it interesting that he never prayed for their problems to go away. He prayed only that they would be strong, patient, and joyful in trials, and that they would endure everything with good temper.

Perhaps we should pray in this way ourselves rather than always praying for God to remove the difficult aspects of our lives.

Thanksgiving increases our faith.

Colossians 2:7 instructs us to be "rooted and built up in him and established in the faith, just as you were taught, abounding in thanksgiving" (ESV). The more thankful we are, the more we recognize God's blessings and providential care in our lives. The more we keep in mind all that God does for us according to His goodness, not according to ours, the more our faith in Him is nourished. We learn from God's Word that faith can grow. Jesus said that some people had little faith and that others had great faith, so obviously faith can grow, and being thankful helps it do so.

Thanksgiving is the expression of joy God-ward, and is therefore a fruit of the Spirit (see Gal. 5:22–23). Believers are encouraged to abound in it (see Col. 2:7). We are not to be a little thankful, but to abound and overflow with thankfulness.

Thanksgiving Is Part of Praise

Praise is defined in the online version of *Vine's Greek New Testament Dictionary* as "a tale [or] narration" that "came to denote 'praise' in the [New Testament] only of praise to God" (gospelhall.org/bible)—that is, a telling or recounting of the good things that God does. Praise is to be ascribed to God, in respect of His *glory* ("the exhibition of His character and operations," according to *Vine's* (gospelhall.org/bible).

The Word repeatedly instructs us to give praise—even to offer God a "sacrifice of praise": "Through him then let us continually offer up a sacrifice of praise to God, that is, the fruit of lips that acknowledge his name" (Heb. 13:15 ESV). A sacrifice often denotes giving up something. This Scripture asks us to give up complaining and instead find something to be thankful for in every situation. Under the Old Covenant the people offered animals and produce as sacrifices to God, but He desires that we bring Him hearts filled with gratitude for all His goodness. When we do, these prayers of thankfulness go up before Him as a sweet-smelling sacrifice, and they please Him.

The devil is the one that tempts us to complain, grumble, murmur, and find fault with our lives, with the people in our lives, and even at times with God. We can resist him and instead be obedient to God in this important area of being thankful and grateful, and saying so!

CHAPTER 18

A Beautiful Mind

I am afraid that, even as the serpent beguiled Eve by his cunning, your minds may be corrupted and led away from the simplicity of [your sincere and] pure devotion to Christ.

2 Corinthians 11:3

I was addicted to reasoning for years. I could not be at peace unless I thought I had everything figured out, and the result was a lot of confusion and complication and a lack of peace.

Christianity is simple, but the devil works to turn it into something complex, difficult, and confusing. We are to be on our guard against our powerful adversary, and anytime we find ourselves confused, we should remember that God is not a God of confusion (see 1 Cor. 14:33). We are to beware so no one will deceive us or take us captive through philosophy (Col. 2:8).

One of God's greatest gifts to humanity is the mind. The ability to understand, think, and contemplate sets us apart from all other creatures. Scriptures in the Book of Proverbs and throughout the Bible urge us repeatedly to seek knowledge, but leaning too heavily on our own knowledge can become dangerous. God wants us to seek knowledge of Him and His principles. Because humanity is fallen, this great gift of the mind and its ability to retain knowledge often make people proud, even to the point that they think they know more than they do. The devil has always attacked people in their thinking. He also attacks our emotions and our will, but our minds are his favorite target. We should seek to keep our minds filled with beautiful, good, peaceful thoughts.

One would suppose that the more intelligent people are, the less likely they are to be deceived, but sometimes the opposite is true. The more simpleminded a person is, the easier it is to think as a little child and simply believe what the Bible says about Christ. Jesus said we must come to Him as little children or we won't enter His Kingdom (see Luke 18:17). In the world, simpleminded people are often mistakenly considered not very intelligent, but in God's Kingdom that is not the case. God desires that we simply believe what He says in His Word above all else. Some people who are very intelligent and depend on their own minds too much may have difficulty believing the gospel because of its simplicity. They think something more complex must be added to it.

Paul was highly educated, and God used him to write two-thirds of the New Testament. There is certainly nothing wrong with being educated. Our minds can be a great advantage to us, but they can also hinder simple faith in Jesus. Paul taught the Greeks, who were also highly educated, and he found it necessary to remind them frequently to be careful of the possible dangers of depending on their knowledge too much (see 1 Cor. 1:22–25). Some people want to understand everything and spend a great deal of time reasoning about matters that are not clear to them. A scientist, for example, might have difficulty believing the simple truth of the Bible because he feels he needs scientific proofs in order to believe. Although we should use our reason, we must also come to the conclusion that reason is not and never will be sufficient to understand the things of God.

Mysteries

There is nothing I enjoy more than a good mystery. Mystery stories intrigue me. Watching and waiting for the plot to unfold can keep me on the edge of my seat. The fact that God is filled with mystery is part of what makes a relationship with Him attractive. For example, the fact that Jesus was born of a virgin is a mystery. The Trinity is a mystery. Christ in us is a mystery that was once hidden but is now revealed (see Col. 1:26–27). The wisest person in the world is the one who understands that he will never understand everything, especially not God and His plan for the redemption of mankind. When it comes to the gospel of Christ, we believe with our hearts, not our heads. We didn't see Christ die on the cross, but in our hearts we believe He did. We don't see Him with our natural eyes, but we know positively that He is with us at all times.

> *The wisest person in the world is the one who understands that he will never understand everything.*

Paul warned the Corinthians that they could be self-deceived. He said people should not deceive themselves by thinking they are wise in the way the world views wisdom, but that they should become fools as far as worldly wisdom is concerned, so they can be truly wise in the things that really matter (see 1 Cor. 3:18). There is worldly wisdom, and there is the wisdom that comes from God. Worldly wisdom and philosophies are what Paul warns us to beware of (see 1 Cor. 1:18–31). A philosopher is one who is a thinker. We all think, but it is possible to think too much and end up reasoning ourselves out of the simple truth of God's Word.

An intelligent person might say it makes no sense that one man could die for the sins of all, or that making yourself last eventually makes you first, or that in order to get more we must give away some of what we have. The more people try to force these mysteries to make sense to the mind, the more confusing they seem. It is at this point of excessive reasoning that Satan can slip in and offer a seemingly reasonable solution. He offers a thought or philosophy that seems to fit neatly into the mind, but it can be filled with dangerous error and lead a person into great deception.

Many who do not believe in God say they cannot believe in a God who would allow the kind of suffering we see in the world. God would not allow little children to starve, they say. But God's Word tells us that God is always and only good and that the problems in the world exist due to humanity's rebellion against God and His plan for mankind (see Rom. 5:12–21). This doesn't mean that children who are starving have been rebellious, but our world is messed up because it is filled with sin, and any truly intelligent person can see that the more sin increases in the world, the more our problems increase also. Many of these situations are mysteries to us. We don't understand why good people have cancer or why a mother loses all four of her children in a house fire.

These types of circumstances are times for us to lean on God and trust Him. They should not become opportunities for us to blame God and then let Satan distance us from Him because we don't understand the reason for the problem. We don't need faith if we have all the answers. Trusting God requires that we allow mysteries and unanswered questions, that we believe God has all the answers, and that we are convinced He is good and just.

Our minds devise plans, but thankfully God directs our steps (see Prov. 16:9). As anyone who has been in relationship with God for any length of time would know, God is filled with surprises and frequently does things that do not make sense to the human mind.

We may reason about many things, but there must be a limit

to our reasoning, a point at which we are satisfied to simply believe something because God said it, and we need nothing else to convince us. I often ponder or reason regarding something until I start to feel confused, and that is my sign that I have gone too far because God is not the author of confusion, the devil is (see 1 Cor. 14:33).

God reveals a great deal to us and it is wonderful when He does, but there are also secrets hidden in Him that we will never understand until we are in Heaven and know all things. Paul writes to the Corinthians that now we know in part, but the day will come when we will know even as we are known; the partial will pass away and perfection will come (see 1 Cor. 13:9–10). However, that won't happen while we are still on Earth.

Deuteronomy 29:29 says that the secret things belong to God and the things that are revealed belong to us. We must be satisfied not to know many things and not allow the "unknowing" to affect our faith adversely. We are privileged to have a faith that goes beyond knowing. We can know truth in our hearts even though our minds say that what we believe makes no sense.

Paul writes, "Great is the mystery of godliness" (1 Tim. 3:16 NKJV). Personally, I am thrilled by the mystery. If we knew everything as God knows it, then I don't see how He could be our God. The very essence of God indicates that He is above us in every way. We are to look up to Him and respect and admire what we don't comprehend about Him with our finite minds. I think life would be rather boring if we knew everything that was going to happen before it happened.

How does this fit into letting God fight our battles? It partially depends on whether or not we can believe what the Word of God says even when life seems to make no sense. If we cannot do that, then we end up fighting battle after battle in our own minds and becoming more and more confused. To have a painful problem is miserable, but to be confused about the problem adds another layer of pain. Psalm 37:3 offers God's answer to problems that seem unfair: "Trust in the LORD, and do good" (ESV). This verse promises that even though the wicked seem to prosper for a time, their end will come and the righteous will inherit the Earth. Faith invites us to look beyond what is happening right now to the glorious future God has promised us.

Reasoning

It is not surprising that when we are hurting, we want to find reasons for what has happened to us. But searching for answers we probably won't get often makes our pain even more intense.

What I do, and suggest to others, is to ask God to show me anything that will help me understand. But if nothing comes to me, then I trust God enough not to have to know why something happened. Also, I trust Him to do as He has promised and work something good out of the tragedy (see Rom. 8:28). Even if God does not give us the answers we would like, He will comfort us because He is the God of all comfort (see 2 Cor. 1:3).

I was once the kind of person who could not be calm and feel safe until I thought I had things figured out. I worried about almost everything I didn't feel I could control. I wanted to understand why things happened and when and how answers would come. I am forever grateful that God has renewed my mind through the study of His Word and has taught me to think thoughts that are beneficial rather than useless.

My mind, like yours, is capable of finding reasons that seem to make sense. Our reasons comfort us for a period of time and often cause us to feel in control of what is happening to us, but in the end we usually find that we were wrong and simply didn't know it.

It is interesting that we feel comforted if we *think* we have life figured out, even though we can be wrong about what we think. Therein lies the danger of going beyond God's Word and finding comfort in human philosophy. You may ask, "How can I ever know if what I believe is truth or deception?" We can know with certainty what truth is by having knowledge of God's Word. Paul writes about this very subject:

> I am astonished that you are so quickly deserting him who called you in the grace of Christ and are turning to a different gospel—not that there is another one, but there are some who trouble you and want to distort the gospel of Christ. But even if we or an angel from heaven should preach to you a gospel contrary to the one we preached to you, let him be accursed.
>
> Galatians 1:6–8 ESV

If the devil cannot get you not to believe in Christ, then he will agree with you that faith in God is fine and good, but that something needs to be added to the simplicity of the gospel. He has operated this way for centuries. For example, he used certain people to tell the Galatian believers that in addition to the gospel of grace, they also needed circumcision (see Gal. 5:1–10). He suggested to them that surely God would not simply forgive all their sins because they believed in Jesus, but if they would add some of their own works to what God had done, they would be doing the right thing. When that teaching started making sense to their minds, Paul chastised them because they had so quickly deserted the truth (see Gal. 3:1–6).

Consider this example: A Christian woman loses her husband in an accident and in her pain she searches for answers, but finds none. A friend at work tells her about a psychic that is amazing and suggests she make an appointment. Even though the Bible clearly warns us against getting advice from such people (see Lev. 19:26), the grieving woman consults the psychic. The psychic gives her some reasons concerning her husband's death that make sense to her mind, and even goes so far as to give the woman a (supposed) message from her deceased husband. Now this woman may feel comforted, but she is deceived. If she feels convicted that what she has done is wrong, she further reasons that God has comforted her through the psychic. Once again she feels comforted, but she is becoming more and more deceived with each lie she believes. She may begin to see the psychic on a regular basis and descend deeper into deception each time she does. Just because something makes sense to our minds does not mean it is good or that it is godly.

Our lives would be so much sweeter and easier if we would simply believe what God says whether it makes sense to our minds or not. Some of us have no problem doing that, but highly intelligent people might. I am not saying they will definitely have problems, but it is a possible danger to watch out for.

If God has given you an exceptional mind, be careful that it doesn't make you proud and, as Paul said, "puffed up" (1 Cor. 13:4 NKJV; Col. 2:18 NKJV). The greater our gifts, the more humble we should be. Gifted public speakers, amazing singers, highly intelligent people, and many other talented individuals need to make sure they realize their gifts are from God and not from themselves. Their abilities make them no better than anyone else; they simply allow them to do something that should be done for God's glory and for no other reason.

Evolutionists may say it is impossible that God created from nothing everything we see in the span of just a few days. But the man or woman of faith reads Hebrews 11:3, which says, "By faith we understand that the worlds were framed by the word of God, so that the things which are seen were not made of things which are visible (NKJV). To the person who walks by faith, evolution makes no sense at all. How can everything we see just accidentally happen over millions of years? If humanity is an accident, then we have no value. But if we are created in the image of God, as the Bible says in Genesis 1:27, then our worth and value are beyond anything we can even imagine.

Satan uses the theory of evolution (and please remember, it is a theory) to steal the knowledge of who we truly are. He wants us to feel worthless and unloved because then he can control us with his lies.

Before you sink too far into reasoning and get yourself into trouble, remember this powerful instruction from Proverbs:

> Trust in the LORD with all your heart, and do not lean on your own understanding. In all your ways acknowledge him, and he will make straight your paths. Be not wise in your own eyes; fear the LORD, and turn away from evil.
>
> Proverbs 3:5–7 ESV

You're Not as Smart as You Think You Are

Instead of simply stating, "You are not as smart as you think you are," the writer of Proverbs says, "Be not wise in your own eyes" (Prov. 3:7 ESV). His words sound more polite, so nice that we may miss the point, so I want to be plain: We are not as smart as we sometimes think we are! We are not the only ones who are always right. We are not always the ones with the best answer. We don't have everything in life figured out. And if we allow ourselves to be deceived into thinking otherwise, Satan has succeeded in one of his most cunning strategies against us.

This doesn't mean we need to think we are dumb or ignorant, but it means that whatever we are good at, it is because of the grace of God alone. Let's pray that our minds will be continually flooded with humility because humility keeps us safe. Those who humble themselves under the hand of God will be exalted in due time (see 1 Pet. 5:6). God can use in mighty ways those who don't think more highly of themselves than they ought to.

Pride was Satan's downfall (see Isa. 14:13–14), and it will be ours also if we allow it into our thinking. Pride causes us to lift ourselves up and put others down, and it causes us to devalue people Jesus deems valuable enough to die for. Pride distorts our thinking to the point where we actually may try to give God advice, as Peter did when he advised Jesus not to go to Jerusalem to be killed (see Matt. 16:21–23).

If you buy into the devil's philosophies and vain deceits, you will be fighting a battle all of your life. But if you will believe God's Word, He will fight your battles for you!

Paul said that the cross is folly to those who do not believe, but to those who are being saved it is the power of God (see 1 Cor. 1:18). Then he quoted from the Old Testament, saying, "I will destroy the wisdom of the wise, and the discernment of the discerning I will thwart" (1 Cor. 1:19 ESV). Paul goes on to make several statements I will paraphrase: He says that God has made foolish the wisdom of the world, because the world could not know God through its wisdom, but it pleased God through the folly of preaching to save those who believe (see 1 Cor. 1:20–21).

It is truly amazing what happens in some people's hearts

when the gospel is being preached. It is as though a light comes on inside of them, and they believe. The words (God's Word) become a reality in their hearts, and they gladly give their lives to Jesus and receive His life into them. No worldly wisdom can do this for a person. God further perplexes those who think they are wise in this world by using people whom the world views as weak and foolish as His instruments, working through them and thereby putting the wise in this world to shame. He does this so people cannot boast in themselves (see 1 Cor. 1:21–31). Christ is our wisdom from God, and as long as we follow Him, we will be wise men and women.

CHAPTER 19

Breaking Satan's Assignment

A man without self-control is like a city broken into and left without walls.

Proverbs 25:28 ESV

Satan is carrying out an assignment against us, but we need not be concerned because we have the power through Christ to break that assignment. Jesus said that the thief (Satan) comes for one purpose—to steal, kill, and destroy (see John 10:10). Whether he wants to steal our dreams for our lives, our confidence, our relationship with God, our friendships, our joy, or our peace, he is a thief!

The One Who is in us is greater than the devil who is in the world (see 1 John 4:4); therefore, we don't need to be afraid of anything he may have planned to harm us. God is for us, so nothing the devil or anyone else tries to do to harm us will ultimately prove successful if we continue to trust and obey God.

We have looked at some ways we can work with the Holy Spirit to keep Satan from gaining entrance into our lives, such as praying, putting on our spiritual armor, using our weapons, refusing to be angry, and being quick to forgive. But there is another important way we haven't explored yet—self-control and discipline.

1 Peter 5:8 teaches us to be well-balanced and self-disciplined because our adversary, the devil, roams around like a hungry lion, seeking someone to devour.

Living a balanced life is impossible without self-control and the ability to discipline our thoughts, emotions, and choices. It also requires regular examination of our lives and asking God to reveal any area that may be out of balance. If He does, it requires us to take action to correct any excess.

I mentioned the need to be well-balanced in chapter 7, but now I would like to discuss it in greater detail. To be balanced, a person must never be extreme in any area, but strive to keep the right balance in every area of life. As stated, this requires diligence and an abundance of self-control and self-discipline. People have often asked me how I keep my priorities straight, considering everything I am doing. I finally found the perfect answer, which is that I am always straightening them out. Just like anyone, I find at times that I am doing too much of one thing and not enough of another. So I make a change for the better, and before long I recognize that the same malady has taken hold of me again in a different area than before. Satan is relentless in finding new ways to gain access into our lives, and exposing that is one reason I wrote this book.

Most people groan when I announce that I am going to teach on the subject of discipline, but without it, we will never become who we truly want to be or do the things we want to do. Satan has an assignment, and part of it is to prevent us from fulfilling our destiny or enjoying any area of our lives. We must be steadfast and determined. Yes, God will fight our battles for us, but we must also do our part, which includes living a well-balanced, disciplined life.

Free Will

God has given us a free will. He will not control us or force us to do the right thing. He will guide, lead, urge, and encourage, but

He will not force us. God wants us to use our free will to choose His will, but whether we do that or not is up to us. Self-control is a fruit of the Spirit (see Gal. 5:22–23), but like all good fruit that comes with the new birth in Christ, it must be developed. The more we use it, the stronger it becomes. We all use self-control to some degree, otherwise we would not accomplish anything, but the more we use it, the more we accomplish.

We are complex beings with minds that think, emotions that feel, and wills that want. We also have bodies that get tired, lazy, and hungry. They don't always cooperate willingly with what we want to do, so we have to use the discipline and self-control God has given us. People who always do what they feel like doing play right into the devil's hand, and if they continue, their lives will amount to nothing. Our feelings are a driving factor in our lives, and we are often tempted to let them rule us, but we must not. Satan uses our feelings against us by causing us to think we must feel like doing something in order to do it, but that is incorrect. We learn to live by principle rather than by our feelings. We should set godly standards for our lives and discipline ourselves to follow them. We cannot follow every thought we think, because many of our thoughts are dropped into our minds by the devil and would lead us down paths of destruction, so we must also discipline our thoughts and control them.

I encourage you to pray that God will show you when your thoughts are going the wrong direction so you can choose to think on something good that will bring life instead of misery to you. Several times each day you may find your mind drifting into areas that will bear no good fruit or may even lead you into sin, but this is not a problem as long as you recognize it as the devil's attempt to get you going in a wrong direction. Then you can simply say, "No, I will not think like this!"

Every area of life requires the use of discipline and self-control in order to remain balanced. At any given time we can slip out of balance in an area simply because we are not paying attention to it. It is very easy to gradually eat a little more and then more and more—and suddenly realize we have gained weight. The reason is that we have not been alert and applying self-control when needed. It is important to learn that our bodies will crave more and more of whatever we give them on a regular basis. If I begin to eat one piece of candy from a box of chocolates every night after dinner, at first just one will satisfy me, but before long my body will crave two and then three—and if I give in to its demands, soon I will have a problem. I will gain weight, eat too much sugar, and perhaps feel bad due to the excess.

The flesh is greedy and cannot be satisfied with anything for very long. We always want more! No matter what a person owns, it can only satisfy them temporarily, and then they crave something new to excite them. We can easily see why we need to use self-control and not depend on our feelings to lead us in the right direction.

We must resist the devil at his onset (see 1 Pet. 5:8–9) and not keep procrastinating about adjusting areas that are out of balance in our lives; the longer we let problems continue, the more difficult it will be to break free from them. People think living a disciplined life means they will never get to do anything they want to do, and the truth is that our flesh won't get to do what it wants to do, but our spirits will be happy and free.

If you think doing whatever you want to do anytime you want to do it is freedom, just look at the lives of people who are doing that. You will see misery and destruction. Perhaps not at first, but eventually the problems will start showing up. The apostle

Paul wrote that he was free to do anything he wanted to do, but that not all things were expedient or the best for him to do, so he disciplined himself and chose the best things (see 1 Cor. 9:27, 10:23). True freedom consists not of doing everything we like, but in having the discipline to do what we should do.

God has given us free will and self-control. To realize that we are not simply assigned a fate that will take place no matter what happens is actually exciting. We have choices about how our lives will turn out, and if we make the right ones, we can live amazingly wonderful lives.

Our Desire to Control

We cannot control God, we cannot control all our circumstances, and we should not try to control other people. But we can and should control ourselves. We have self-control!

Stop trying to do what you can never do, and start doing what you can do. Think about how much less stress you would feel if you stopped trying to control things you cannot control and learned instead how to control yourself.

You cannot make people you care about fall in love with Jesus simply because you love Him. You can pray and be a good example for them, but you can't force them. Joshua told the people that they should choose for themselves who they would serve, and that he and his house would serve the Lord (see Josh. 24:15). You can't force people who are born with easygoing, laid-back personalities to be more aggressive. You can't force your children to fulfill your unfulfilled dreams, but you must help them be who God has designed them to be. You can't control people; you have to give them freedom of choice. That is what God does for us.

In Deuteronomy 30:19, He says, "I call heaven and earth to witness against you today, that I have set before you life and death, blessing and curse. Therefore choose life, that you and your offspring may live" (ESV).

When our children are very young, we make decisions for them, but as they grow older we must gradually relinquish some of that control and help them learn to make good decisions according to God's will, not according to our will or to their own will.

The main reason we try to control circumstances and people is that we are selfish and afraid we won't get what we want. We may also be controlling because we have been hurt or treated unjustly in the past and we are merely trying to protect ourselves. Either way, we need to stop trying to control things that are not ours to control and trust God to do what is right for us.

Practicing Self-Control

As I stated, what God wants us to control is ourselves. This is the only way to maintain a balanced life and prevent the devil from taking advantage of us. I'm not sure many people would think being out of balance is a way for the devil to gain entrance into our lives, but it is.

Let's think about the importance of self-control in several aspects of your everyday life. You know that the enemy attacks your spiritual life, your thoughts, and even your relationships, but he does not limit his attacks to those areas. He will harass you in any possible way, including in practical matters such as your words, your finances, your time, and your appetite. Exercising self-control in these aspects of your life will help defeat him.

Words

Do you talk too much? Many will answer yes to that question, but there is another way we may be out of balance concerning talking, which is that we may talk too little. Although quietness is preferred over excessive talkativeness, some people are so quiet that they make others uncomfortable. Some people may need to discipline themselves to listen more and talk less, but some need to discipline themselves to talk a little more. Some people won't speak up even when they need to. They allow others to take advantage of them because they don't like to confront people who are behaving badly. If the Holy Spirit prompts us to confront someone in an attitude of love and we refuse because we are uncomfortable with it, we are just as guilty as those who confront everyone they don't agree with even when the Holy Spirit is urging them to be quiet.

I once allowed a man I worked for to control my time, and I did not say anything about it. No matter what I had planned, if he decided to call a meeting or have a staff dinner, he expected me to drop everything and do as he wished. He exhibited other similar behavior, and after I finally left the job, feeling bitter because he had controlled me, God spoke to my heart that although this man was wrong in controlling people and being inconsiderate, I was just as guilty for letting him do it. I should have spoken up, but I kept quiet out of fear of losing my job. There is a time to be silent and a time to speak, and the balanced person knows the difference.

Finances

What about finances? Do you spend too much and purchase unnecessary items or things that get you into debt and ultimately pressure you? If so, then you need to discipline yourself to spend less and use prudence in managing the resources God has given you. On the other hand, there are some people who do not spend enough money. They are so focused on saving for the future that they never enjoy the present. They are what others call tightwads. One man said of another, "That man is tighter than the bark on a tree." The man had grown up in poverty and had allowed the devil to cause him to fear not having enough. In the process he sacrificed some legitimate things God wanted him and his family to enjoy.

People who refuse to do anything for themselves often end up feeling deprived even though they are responsible for it. If these people have families, the family members usually resent the rigid attitude toward spending. We should be balanced, and a good plan is to save some, give some, and spend some of our increase. This plan, if followed, will keep you out of trouble with finances, and will also allow you to enjoy the fruit of your labors.

Time

Another area of concern is time. We should not waste our time, but neither should we feel that we must constantly be productive. We need work, rest, play, and worship. I tend toward working too much, and that has caused me physical problems in the past. Anyone who works too much will end up with stress, and chronic stress can cause unimaginable health problems and trouble in other areas of our lives. I have to be very attentive to the Holy Spirit's guidance in this area, and I find myself regularly making adjustments in order to stay balanced. However, I know other people who are basically lazy or passive, and they waste most of their time and do very little with the gifts and opportunities God has given them. They also need to discipline themselves.

Appetite

One final area I will mention is appetite. Multitudes of people, especially those in Western cultures, are not only overweight, but the types of food they choose to eat are unhealthy. Our bodies are temples of the Holy Spirit (see 1 Cor. 6:19), and as such we should discipline ourselves to be healthy houses for Him to dwell in. Not everyone will be skinny, just as not everyone will be tall, but we should maintain balance concerning food, and eat and enjoy what we need without overeating. This is not meant to condemn people who weigh more than they should, but it is an encouragement to value yourself enough to be as healthy as you can be.

Food is a great temptation to many people and understandably so. It tastes good and seems to be pushed in front of us almost everywhere we go. Rather than focusing on losing weight or being on a diet, I encourage people to focus on being healthy. I believe that as you choose healthy food in right proportions, you will ultimately weigh what is right for your body type and metabolism.

I could talk about many areas of life when it comes to the subject of self-control because every area of life needs to be disciplined and controlled or it will get out of balance and give the devil an opportunity. Discipline is your friend, not your enemy, and it will keep you in balance and help you live the life you truly want to live.

Just think of the areas I mentioned and how miserable people can be if they don't discipline their thoughts, their speech, their spending, the use of their time, and their appetites. The discomfort of discipline pales in comparison to the ultimate discomfort of being undisciplined. I guess we might say, "Pick your pain: Endure the temporary pain of discipline and self-control, or endure the endless pain and misery of guilt, sickness, stress, debt, and wasting your time."

I believe God has given us self-control as a gift to help us live balanced lives, and I urge you to value the gift.

CHAPTER 20

Internal Rest

"Take my yoke upon you, and learn from me, for I am gentle and lowly in heart, and you will find rest for your souls."

Matthew 11:29 ESV

In December 2017 I suddenly became very ill. My mouth was extremely dry and my blood pressure was high. I felt shaky, had shortness of breath, and lost my appetite. Of course I went to my doctor, who found no apparent problem, so I went to two other doctors who specialize in certain areas, and they found no problem. I was understandably frustrated because I felt really bad and was losing weight rapidly. I asked a doctor who is also a minister and a friend to put me in the hospital for a few days and run all the tests necessary to find out what was wrong. When all the tests came back stating I was very healthy, and medical professionals said they had never seen blood work as good as mine in anyone my age, I asked, "Well, what is wrong with me?"

I was told I had adrenal fatigue and chronic stress from working too hard for too long and that I needed some long-term rest and changes in lifestyle. The doctors emphasized that I needed to learn how to rest internally. In others words, I was to let my mind and emotions be at rest, not just my physical body.

What do I do while I rest?

My first question was, "What do I do while I rest?" This question shows why I had a problem, but I have discovered that many people are in similar situations. During the time that has gone by since that diagnosis, I have learned how to schedule my life better, accepted the fact that I cannot always do what I have always done, and come to understand that I must be willing to make changes.

It is fairly easy to adjust our schedules to enable ourselves to get more physical rest, but we can lie on a beach in the sun all day and still not rest because we are not resting our souls. We can be in bed and still worry, trying to figure out solutions to problems or endeavoring to fix situations that are not even our responsibilities.

Much of how we handle our lives internally is initially determined by our temperament, but we can and must learn balance. Being a type A, choleric personality, I tend to be very busy inside. But thankfully, God has shown me a great deal since December 2017, and I am doing well at this point in my life. I am able to fulfill all of my responsibilities, but I am doing them while resting internally. I trust God more and depend on myself less.

As I have shared my story with others, almost without exception people whose temperaments are similar to mine have asked me the same question I asked the doctor: "How do you rest?" The kind of rest Jesus offers us is not rest *from* work but rest *in* work. It is not an invitation to lie on the sofa all day and do nothing; it is an invitation to accomplish a great deal, but to do it in peace.

The more we can develop and maintain the type of rest Jesus offers us, the easier life becomes and the more we release God to fight our battles for us instead of always feeling like we are personally fighting something.

The devil does all he can to keep us from understanding and entering true Sabbath rest. Hebrews 4 teaches us that the promise of entering God's rest still remains (v. 9), and that those who believe can enter it. Scripture encourages us to "*strive* to enter that rest" (Heb. 4:11 ESV; italics mine), and when we do, we cease from our works of the flesh (see Heb. 4:10).

To "strive to enter" indicates that we may have to learn some new lessons, change some of our ways, and make an effort to do things differently. I still have a lot to learn about this, but I want to share some of what I have learned about resting internally. I hope that it will help you as you go forward, learning how to let God fight your battles because they belong to Him.

Worry

I have written about worry in previous chapters, but I want to say more about it here. Worry is useless, but most of us continue to do it, especially in certain areas, until we finally realize that the longer we worry, the longer we delay the help God wants to give us. If we truly believe that our battles belong to the Lord, then we must remain peaceful. I urge you to pay more attention to what is going on inside of you. Your private thoughts and feelings about what is happening in your life at any given time can cause stress and steal your peace. Often we spend hours worrying, rotating our minds around and around problems, searching for answers without even realizing we are doing it. If you feel your neck and shoulder muscles getting tense, or if your stomach begins to hurt, the first thing to do is to consider what you have been thinking about.

Worry produces physical symptoms that can be a blessing because they alert us to the fact that we are worrying. Then we can ask God to help us and we can choose to cast our care on Him (see 1 Pet. 5:7). Don't forget that God told the Israelites to hold their peace and He would fight for them (see Exod. 14:13–14).

One thing we must do in order not to worry is to learn to deal with our lives as they are and not as we would like them to be. The same approach goes for the people in our lives. We must learn to love them as they are, and not the way we would like them to be. Some of the writers from the sixteenth and seventeenth centuries wrote about "acceptance with joy," meaning that if a situation wasn't going to change, they learned to accept it and remain joyful. Doing so doesn't mean nothing will ever change, but it does mean that for the present time, we trust God's will and timing in every situation. We simply cannot base our joy and peace on our circumstances. If we do, the devil can manipulate them continually, causing us to be upset most of the time. Whatever we might be going through at any given time will pass, and until it does, we can decide to enjoy our lives and keep our peace.

Paul wrote to the Corinthians that his desire was for them to be free from all distressing care, which would require learning to deal with life as it was (see 1 Cor. 7:27–35).

We show humility by casting our care on God. When we refuse to worry, we are saying in essence, "I know I cannot solve this problem, but I trust that God can." Then He goes to work on our behalf, and we experience the benefits of letting Him fight our battles for us.

Dave always says, "Do your responsibility; cast your care." I think that is why Paul instructs us to do everything the crisis demands and

> Do your responsibility; cast your care.

then stand firmly in our place (see Eph. 6:13). We cannot do any more than we can do, and when we try to go beyond that point we become frustrated and lose our peace.

Ask yourself right now if there is anything you can do about any situation in your life that is frustrating you. If the answer is, "No, I can't," then cast your care, keep your joy, and let God do what you cannot do.

By nature I would tend to be a worrier because I am a "fixer." I want to fix problems. Nothing is more frustrating to me than a problem I cannot fix, so I have had to learn to take the same advice I am offering to you.

False Sense of Responsibility

Many people live with a false, or an overactive, sense of responsibility. They feel responsible for things for which they are not responsible. In fact, continually fixing things for other people may hinder them from learning to handle their own problems. The tendency toward false responsibility is partially a temperament trait, but it still needs to be dealt with.

I am a very responsible person. If you give me a job to do it will get done, but often I drift out of my lane and make myself responsible for other people's problems when I should be saving my energy and mental space for my own situations.

Recently, I learned this in a rather cute and funny way, but it did teach me the lengths I go to in finding ridiculous situations to be concerned about. I was in the nail salon getting my nails done and two women came in together, both wanting a pedicure. Only one technician was available at the time, and he took the ladies to the pedicure stations and let them put their feet in warm water. He proceeded to work on one of them, but never said anything to the other lady about when someone would be available to work on her, so I became concerned about her. I am a communicator, and the fact that no one was communicating with her bothered me.

Then three more people came into the salon and were told to sign in and have a seat. They were not informed how long they might have to wait, so I grew concerned about them. I found myself looking around the shop at the workers, trying to determine how soon technicians would be available for the waiting customers. I suddenly realized what I was doing, and it was almost laughable. This situation, which I allowed, caused me ten minutes of internal stress over a situation that was none of my business, nor was it my responsibility.

The incident at the nail salon has helped me learn to stay in my own lane, and I hope it will help you, too. Whether you are still taking responsibility for grown children, friends, or people you don't even know, I recommend that you reconsider what the stress of over-responsibility may be doing to you while not producing any positive results.

Just as I found myself internally trying to run the nail shop more efficiently, perhaps you are trying to do something that is not only frustrating you but keeping you from doing what you should be doing.

Anything God wants us to do will work, and we can do it peacefully. When that good fruit of peace is not present, we are probably trying to do something that is not ours to do.

Anxiety

When we are anxious, we use the time God has given us today to try to fix or solve something that is either in the past or in the future. All we can do with the past, especially regarding mistakes we have made, is to repent, make restitution when possible, learn from the mistakes, and then let them go and move on with our lives.

There is no reason to be anxious about the future, because it isn't here yet, and we have no guarantee that it will be. This is why God's Word teaches us that each day has sufficient trouble of its own and we should not worry about tomorrow (see Matt. 6:34). We may need to make certain plans and preparations for the future, but being anxious about them is useless.

I have lost a great deal of my life spending the present day living in the past or in the future. I don't do that now, but I did for many years, and I pray you will not do as I did. Although there are many things I wish I had done differently, I cannot go back and redo them, so I refuse to lose another day being anxious and worried about them. God can fight the battles of our past mistakes and actually work them for our good if we will release them to Him.

> God can fight the battles of our past mistakes and actually work them for our good.

I believe God has a good future planned for all of us, and we should look forward to it with anticipation and joy, not with fear and anxiety. All storms are not in the weather forecast. Storms we don't expect and may not want in our lives will come, but God's grace is sufficient to help us deal with them.

I recently spoke with a Christian woman who told me that her fourteen-year-old son had his leg amputated because of bone cancer. Her attitude was joyful and could not have been any better. She said that she expected God to use this circumstance in her son's life to make him a better man and to help others.

She and her son faced an unexpected, unwanted problem, but they chose an attitude that would glorify God and release Him to fight their battle. We can remember that our battles belong to the Lord and let Him fight them, or we can fight them ourselves. If we want to win them, we need to release our worries, our anxieties, and all other frustrating emotions to God and hold on to our peace while we wait for victory.

Trust God and Enjoy Each Day

None of us knows how long we have left to live. We trust God for long and healthy lives, but how long we live is ultimately up to Him. We may do foolish things that shorten our lives, but only God can lengthen them. No matter how much time we have, we should maximize it by enjoying it, holding on to our peace, and being more than conquerors through a personal relationship with Jesus. This only happens as we learn to do what we can do and trust God to do what we cannot do.

God wants to—and will—fight our battles for us. Without Him, we won't win them anyway, but we have to release them to Him if we want the victory only He can give. I pray that you will receive His grace to enable you to do just that so you will be free to enjoy each moment of every day.

CHAPTER 21

Protecting Yourself from Satan, the Thief

"The thief comes only to steal and kill and destroy. I came that they may have life and have it abundantly."

John 10:10 ESV

The Bible refers to Satan as a thief, and the main thing he wants to steal or prevent is our relationship with God through Christ. He doesn't mind if we follow some form of religion, because that usually amounts only to a list of rules and regulations we attempt to follow, thinking it will put us in good standing with God. Jesus did not die for us so we could have some brand of religion, and there is a large variety to choose from; He died so we could have an intimate, personal relationship with God through Him.

When I ask people if they are Christians and they respond by telling me what religion they are, it concerns me. No matter what religion we are, it doesn't save us—only true faith in Jesus does that.

When some of the disciples asked what they needed to do to be working the works of God, or to please Him, Jesus answered, "This is the work of God, that you believe in Him whom He sent" (John 6:29 NKJV). Believing this is the only requirement is difficult for us. We think that surely we must add some good works just to be sure we are accepted.

We are supposed to do good works, but we don't do them to gain acceptance or love from God. We do them because in His grace and mercy, He has provided acceptance to us as an unconditional gift. Our obedience should be a response to God's goodness, not an effort to gain anything from Him.

> *Our obedience should be a response to God's goodness, not an effort to gain anything from Him.*

Satan delights in deceiving people in this area. By doing so, he can turn people into legalists—people who work hard to follow every rule, make sure they read certain amounts of Scripture daily, pray for specified lengths of time and do good works, but sadly, do it all with the wrong motive.

Legalism Leads to a Life of Struggle

Works of the flesh produce struggle. They are our human effort trying to do God's job. Our works can't justify us, because Jesus has already done that through His sacrifice on the cross.

I remember the agony of my struggles in the early years of my walk with God. I truly loved the Lord, but Satan had deceived me through the lies he told me about my duty as a Christian. I thought, as millions of others do, that regular church attendance, reading the Bible a little each day, and saying some prayers, along with confessing my sins, summed up what I needed to do. I also believed I needed to do some good works, so I joined the evangelism team of our church. But God had not given me the grace for door-to-door evangelism, so I dreaded it every week.

I felt guilty all the time because the devil made sure I was fully aware of every tiny mistake I made. He is the chief legalist, so he brought to my attention right away any infraction of the rules. Even though I confessed and asked for forgiveness for it, I still felt guilty. Satan is the accuser, and he stays busy accusing us of things we have done wrong or ways in which we are lacking. Jesus wants us to have joy and to enjoy life, but the thief, Satan, comes to steal our joy and our enjoyment.

> *Jesus wants us to have joy and to enjoy life, but the thief, Satan, comes to steal our joy and our enjoyment.*

I tried so hard to change myself, but every effort failed, and I struggled and stayed frustrated continually by disappointment.

> For all who depend on the Law [seeking justification and salvation by obedience to the Law and the observance of rituals] are under a curse.
>
> Galatians 3:10

We cannot change ourselves, but the Bible says, "I am sure of this, that he who began a good work in you will bring it to completion at the day of Jesus Christ" (Phil. 1:6 ESV). God is working in us all the time, and He changes us in varying degrees as we cooperate with the Holy Spirit's work in us. This is an ongoing process and will be completed when Christ returns, for "in the twinkling of an eye" we shall all be changed (see 1 Cor. 15:52). I suggest you learn to be pleased with your progress rather than feel discouraged and guilty about how far you still have to go.

Guilt is one way the devil oppresses us because it places on us a burden that actually prevents us from making progress. Romans 8:1–2 teaches us that there is no longer any condemnation to those who are in Christ Jesus, and that the law of the Spirit of life in Christ has set us free from the law of sin and death.

The Old Covenant required people to follow rules and regulations and to make sacrifices for their sins, but Jesus offers us a

New Covenant under which the law is written in our hearts (see Heb. 8:10). We can now follow the Holy Spirit and be assured of doing the right thing. He has given us His Spirit and has put His heart in us. He is the one and only sacrifice that was ever needed for all time. When we fail, we no longer need to try to do good things to make up for our mistakes. All we need to do is look to the cross of Calvary, where Jesus paid for our sins once and for all (see Heb. 9:12). Under the New Covenant, when we confess our sins and turn from them, He forgives them, forgets them, and remembers them no more (see Heb. 8:12, 10:16–18).

When Jesus was dying on the cross, He said, "It is finished" (John 19:30). What was finished? The system of the law was finished. He kept the law perfectly because we never could, and He instituted a new system we can follow. It gives salvation, righteousness, peace, and joy rather than struggle. We still keep the moral law, but the law of rituals, rules and regulations, and sacrifices has been fulfilled. The moral law is written in our hearts. As believers in Christ, we instinctively know right from wrong.

I like to say that Jesus gave me a new "want-to." The law says we *have to*, but grace gives us a desire to do what's right. It gives us the want-to, and when all is said and done, people end up doing what they want to do most of the time.

When people say to me, "I wanted to call, but I just didn't have the time," they are not telling the truth. The truth is that they wanted to, but not enough to actually follow through and do it. We can find the time to do the things that are truly important to us, and when we do them, they are not burdensome.

We don't have to go to church; we want to. We don't have to pray; we see prayer as a privilege. We don't have to read and study God's Word; we do it because we want to know how God wants us to live.

If you pay attention to your own conversation, you will probably find it filled with "I have to." You may say, "I have to go to the grocery store," but you don't really have to go; you go because you want to eat. Why not say, "I am going to the grocery store," or "I need to go," or "I want to go"? The devil has trained us to say, "I have to" about most things because those very words make us feel we are under pressure.

Jesus never used language like this and neither did the apostles, so I think it would be good for us to retrain ourselves in this area and realize that we do things because we are free to do them. We don't do good works because we have to do them to get God to accept us. We do them because we have God's nature in us, and He is good.

Those who live under the law are always frustrated simply because God will not allow us to get what we want from Him through our own struggle and effort. He requires that we come to Him in faith.

> Without faith it is impossible to please him, for whoever would draw near to God must believe that he exists and that he rewards those who seek him.
>
> Hebrews 11:6 ESV

Christianity is a life of faith, not one of works and effort. Jesus wants us to enjoy our lives and be at peace, but Satan wants to steal everything good that Jesus died to give us.

Pretenders and Hypocrites

The most religious people of Jesus' day were the Pharisees, and He had harsh words to say to them and about them. He said they were like whitewashed tombs, beautiful on the outside but full of dead people's bones (see Matt. 23:27).

The whole of Matthew 23 gives us a clear picture of how Jesus felt about people like the Pharisees, who followed rules and regulations but had no real relationship with God. He told them that they stayed busy telling others what to do but did not do those things themselves. They tied up heavy loads and put heavy burdens on people, yet would not lift a finger to help them. They did their good deeds so other people would see them, not to glorify God. They also loved titles and seats of honor. Jesus actually said that they kept people out of the Kingdom of God rather than helping people get in. He said they never failed to tithe on every little thing they had but omitted the weightier matters such as truly helping people. He said they strained at a gnat and swallowed a camel. They might well correct others for some tiny infraction of the law while committing huge sins themselves. He pronounced woe on them several times. Simply hearing the word *woe* tells me I don't want any of it!

Religion is one of the devil's favorite deceptions. He can use it to fill people with pride over their supposed good works, while filling their hearts with criticism and judgment toward others. What Satan fears most is our having an intimate, personal relationship with God in which we include Him in every area of our lives, and we actually live for, through, and by Him. That is very different from belonging to a religious order or denomination, following a few religious rules and going to church once a week.

God looks at our hearts much more than He looks at our performance. He desires that we love Him with all of our hearts, minds, and wills, and that we do all that we do for Him because we love Him. He wants us to desire His companionship and realize that we cannot do anything without Him.

God gave Moses Ten Commandments, but by the time Jesus came the Pharisees had turned them into no less than 2,200 rules for people to follow. No wonder the people were internally and externally worn out! What relief it must have been when Jesus said, "Come to me...and I will give you rest" (Matt. 11:28 ESV).

Religion is often about what *we* can do, not about what *Jesus* has done. It may focus on religious doctrine rather than on the practice of the gospel in our everyday lives. Of course, we all need sound doctrine, but any organization that teaches only doctrine and never gets around to the practical side of Christianity will produce only frustrated church members who know rules but have no power to follow them. It will produce people with a lot of knowledge but no victory in their lives.

I have studied and written books on Paul's epistles, and I have seen clearly how the first portion of each one focuses on our doctrine, teaching us who we are in Christ and what we should believe. But the second parts of Paul's letters teach us what we should do in light of who we are in Christ and what we believe. If our faith is based on nothing but doctrine, we end up preaching to people but never showing them anything worth following. We need to let people see Jesus through us.

I ask you to examine your motives and make certain you are doing what you do for the right reasons, not merely to be seen, noticed, or well thought of. Be sure you are doing what you do because you believe God wants you to and because you love Him, and not in order to try to gain something from Him.

Where Is the Power?

The apostle Paul wrote to Timothy about people who hold a form of religion, yet "they deny and reject and are strangers to the power of it" (2 Tim. 3:5 AMPC). Being a Christian should be a powerful experience. Paul also prayed that he would know Christ and the power of His resurrection, which lifted him out from among the dead while still in the body (see Phil. 3:10 AMPC). This is the kind of power we should also experience.

As believers in Christ, we should have the power to endure hardship without losing our joy or complaining. We should be able to go through difficult days and still hold on to our peace. We should be able to help

> *As believers in Christ, we should have the power to endure hardship without losing our joy or complaining.*

others while enduring personal trials of our own. We should be quick to forgive and plentiful in mercy. Jesus came to give us power to live ordinary, everyday life in powerful ways others will notice and want to know about.

We can read and observe in the Acts of the Apostles how powerful the early church was. It was a lot different from what we experience today! Not only did those believers witness healings and other miracles, but they also endured great persecution while still remaining joyful. Today it is difficult for us to maintain joy if we are even mildly inconvenienced.

Perhaps we have too much religion and not enough of an intimate relationship with Jesus. It is wise to ask yourself if you are enjoying a close relationship with God or if you are merely going through religious rituals and trying to be a good person. I can personally testify that I was in church regularly for many years before ever hearing anything about the importance of having a personal, intimate relationship with the Lord. He doesn't simply want us to attend church once a week and pay no attention to Him the rest of the time. He wants to be involved in every area of our lives and to have a conversational relationship with us.

I always believed that God was powerful, but I never thought I was or could be powerful also. That unbelief caused me to put up with whatever the devil threw at me, not even realizing it was the devil because I had not heard enough about him to realize he was the source of my problems.

Earlier, we looked at Ephesians 6:10, which tells us to "be strong in the Lord [be empowered through your union with Him]" (AMPC). To be in union with someone means to be one with and to fellowship with. Marriage is often referred to as "the marriage union," but how can two people enter into that without having a rich life of fellowship with one another?

Called to Fellowship with Christ

Our entire experience with God is changed for the better when we realize that what He wants more than anything is for us to love Him and to want to spend time with Him.

> God is faithful, by whom you were called into the fellowship
> of his Son, Jesus Christ our Lord.
>
> 1 Corinthians 1:9 ESV

God calls and invites us into fellowship with Himself, not to struggle to keep the laws, rules, and regulations set by a religious organization. I am not saying that we should avoid incorporating spiritual disciplines into our lives, because doing so is important, but the power to follow guidelines and make right choices comes from our relationship with Jesus.

Religion without relationship becomes a heavy burden. Many religious people are prideful, judgmental, self-righteous, and sour. They have a gloom or heaviness about them that is evident in their expressions and is visible to those

Religion without relationship becomes a heavy burden.

around them. They don't enjoy life, and they usually resent those who do.

But a close relationship with Jesus relieves burdens. As we fellowship with Him, He fights our battles for us. Jesus said that His "yoke is easy [to bear]" and His "burden is light" (Matt. 11:30 AMPC). Anything He asks us to do, He gives us the power to do it, so obeying Him can be a pleasure instead of pressure.

The more we include Jesus in our everyday lives, the more He fights our battles and the less trouble we have with the enemy. Remember, God is never more than one thought away. He is always present, and we need to form a habit of paying attention to Him. We should think of our relationship with Him like this: We don't live in a home with other people and never talk to them. We share with them; we live life with them and enjoy them.

Let me conclude this chapter by saying that merely being religious always produces guilt and condemnation because there is always some rule or law we are unable to keep. Then guilt weighs heavily on us, and we try harder to be a better person, but somehow we always fail.

True religion based on relationship with Jesus helps people. It is always looking for opportunities to help those who are afflicted in any way, and it remains "uncontaminated by the [secular] world" (see James 1:27).

Try focusing on your relationship with the Lord more than on keeping rules and laws, and you will find that the desire to do the right thing will begin to fill your heart and you will do what is right with ease. Don't let the devil steal the relationship with God that Jesus died for you to have and enjoy.

CHAPTER 22

God Always Gives Us the Victory

*Many hardships and perplexing circumstances confront
the righteous, but the LORD rescues him from them all.*

Psalm 34:19

Although we do go through many difficulties in life, we can take
comfort in God's promise to give us victory (see 1 Cor. 15:57). We
can always have hope, which is the confident expectation that
something good is going to happen in our lives.

God does not author our suffering. He delivers us from it when
we trust and obey Him. Satan is the one behind all the misery and
suffering in the world. He is an invisible foe that wreaks havoc in
people's lives mainly because they don't realize that he is their real
problem. I told someone yesterday that I was writing a book that
I hoped would help people recognize when the devil is at work in
their lives and he said, "Chapter One: 'The Devil is a Liar,' Chapter
Two: 'The Devil is a Liar,' Chapter Three: 'The Devil is a Liar.'"

Because the devil is a liar and the father of all lies (see John 8:44),
and is incapable of telling the truth, he craftily puts thoughts into
our minds. Therefore, we must be very careful about what we think.

Satan provokes times of pain and misery in our lives and wants
to use them to discourage us and draw us away from God. He
will attempt to make us think God doesn't love us, especially if
the suffering lasts a long time.

Satan will also attempt to make us think we have sinned in some way, so God must be punishing us through our suffering. Although there are times when hidden personal sin can open a door for Satan to wreak havoc in our lives, that is not always the case. We live in a world full of sin and its results, and Jesus tells us we will have tribulation in the world (see John 16:33). Nowhere does Scripture promise us a life free from suffering. We do, however, have the promise that God will be with us always, that He will rescue us, and that He will work good out of all things if we love Him and want His will (see Rom. 8:28).

Focusing on God's promises in the midst of suffering is very important and will keep us from becoming discouraged. I recall a time when I was sick for a few months and had to resist the fear that I would never get well. When we are in pain, Satan loves to whisper, "What if this never ends?"

When you are suffering, remember that it will come to an end. You are passing through something and it can make you stronger if you allow it to do so. Suffering is a time to exercise your faith and trust in God. I caution you not to spend too much time trying to figure out why you are going through whatever you are going through. The good news is that you're going *through*. You will come out on the other side.

During times of turmoil it helps to remember that you are not alone in your suffering. God is with you. Here is God's promise:

> "When you pass through the waters, I will be with you;
> and through the rivers, they shall not overwhelm you;
> when you walk through fire you shall not be burned, and
> the flame shall not consume you."
>
> Isaiah 43:2 ESV

It also helps to remember that Jesus knows exactly how you feel because He suffered in all ways, just as we do (see Heb. 4:15). He sympathizes with us, and we can draw near to Him and receive the power we need to help us in times of need (see Heb. 4:16).

The devil will shout that you are not going to make it, that you can't stand it, it is too much for you. That is when you say, "I can do all things through Christ who is my strength" (see Phil. 4:13). Putting your trust in God during trials and tribulations releases Him to fight your battles for you.

Discouragement

Discouragement is one of the devil's goals. He wants us to feel downcast in our emotions; he wants our thoughts to be negative and to spiral downward; and he wants our hope to be down. There is nothing "up" about the devil; everything is down. Even our posture can get down. When we are discouraged, we hang our heads low and even our arms hang down. The author of Hebrews writes, "Strengthen the hands which hang down" (Hebrews 12:12 NKJV). People who accomplish great things in life must always face discouragement head-on and move past it courageously.

Our problems often begin with a disappointment. If we dwell on the disappointment long enough, we become discouraged, and then we may go from discouragement to depression to despair. This downward progression is not good. People in despair can be easily tempted to give up. They see no way out of their situations and come to believe their trouble will never end.

When Jesus ascended to the right hand of the Father, He sent us an Encourager, the Holy Spirit, to represent Him and work with us on His behalf (see John 14:26). The Holy Spirit is also called the Comforter (see John 15:26). He is with us to help us, to counsel and to comfort us. He will keep us from discouragement if we will listen to Him. He may encourage us directly in some way or He may—and often does—work through other people to encourage us. God has an antidote for every evil thing the enemy tries to do. All we need to do is discover what it is and apply it in our lives. The devil discourages, but the Holy Spirit encourages. The devil tries to destroy, but God restores, renews, and rebuilds. The devil is a liar, but God is Truth.

You may be thinking, *I wish I had someone to encourage me but I don't.* When the people were talking of stoning King David, he encouraged himself in the Lord (see 1 Sam. 30:6). Likewise, we can encourage ourselves by remembering God's promises to deliver and heal us, and by recalling times in the past when we were suffering and God delivered us. When we remember everything God has brought us through, it is easier to believe we will prevail through our present troubles.

When David was downcast he talked to himself, and I have mentioned previously that talking to yourself can be very valuable. David said: "Why are you cast down, O my soul, and why are you in turmoil within me? Hope in God; for I shall again praise him, my salvation and my God" (Psalm 42:5–6 ESV).

Notice that David said, "I shall" praise the Lord. Perhaps he did not feel like doing it, but he chose to do it. He spoke to himself. You might say he talked himself right out of a bad mood. Think about it: You can talk yourself into a bad mood or you can talk yourself out of one.

> You can talk yourself into a bad mood or you can talk yourself out of one.

In Psalms 42:11 and 43:5, David spoke the same words to himself again. This indicates to me that he struggled with feeling downcast more than once in his life, or perhaps the same episode hung on for a few days and he had to persist in his determination not to let the downcast feelings control him.

Always remember that the devil is persistent, and we will need to be equally persistent if we intend to overcome him. We all have different temperaments, and some people are simply more melancholy or negative than others. These individuals are more easily discouraged than others. Some are inclined to notice every feeling they have and examine it closely. They want to feel good all the time, and when they don't, they dwell on how they feel until they become discouraged. I try not to pay attention to every little feeling I have, because what we pay attention to usually becomes the largest thing in our lives and can seem much bigger than it actually is. If we keep thinking about the pain in our toe, the headache we have, or the disappointment of not getting the promotion we wanted at work, it only makes the pain worse. We need to go out and do something to get our minds off of our problems and trust God to fight our battles for us.

One minister said that the most prevalent problem in the church today is discouragement. One reason for this is the state of the world. We live in difficult and discouraging times. The devil is behind all the problems in the world, and he uses them to the maximum extent. He uses the very problems he has created to discourage us.

Many Psalms are directed at this problem of discouragement, so it must have been a prevalent problem among people in every era. Discouragement can have many causes. As mentioned, it can be a matter of temperament, and in that case, it is very wise to know yourself. Actually, whether you are an extrovert or an introvert, happy and bubbly all the time or easily downcast, it is wise to know yourself. You need not feel discouraged by your weaknesses, but you do need to know what they are. Knowing yourself will help you guard against letting Satan take advantage of you. If you never get to know yourself, you will never be able to live with yourself very well. I do caution you, however, not to be too introspective, because the devil can also take advantage of that by tempting you to focus excessively on what you think your faults are and then become worried and upset about them.

> *If you never get to know yourself, you will never be able to live with yourself very well.*

The Lord knows our frame, and He is mindful that we are but dust (see Ps. 103:14). God is not surprised by our weaknesses; He knew about each of them before we did, and He is prepared to let His strength flow through them if we let Him. While knowing and examining ourselves is right and important, we should also remember that the devil always tries to drive us to extremes. Once again we see the importance of staying balanced. To refuse to recognize our faults is dangerous, but to focus on them too much is also dangerous.

Always remember that you are justified before God because of faith in Jesus Christ (see Gal. 2:16), not because you have no weaknesses. When the devil gives you a list of your faults you may say to him, "Yes, that is all true, but I am justified by faith in Jesus Christ, and I am cleansed by His blood." The devil may whisper to you or he may shout at you; he may work through people who happily point out everything that is wrong with you, but God has already accepted you in the Beloved (see Eph. 1:6) and has promised never to reject those who believe.

God did not send His Son into the world to condemn us for our faults. Whoever believes in Him is not condemned (see John 3:18).

Why Would God Want *Me?*

I'm not perfect. I have all kinds of problems. I have no ability. I have no gifts. I'm just not worthy. Why would God want me?

Well, did you know that...

Moses stuttered.

David's armor didn't fit.

John Mark deserted Paul.

Timothy had ulcers.

Hosea's wife was a prostitute.

Amos' only training was in the school of fig-tree pruning.

Jacob was a liar.

David had an affair.

Abraham was too old.

David was too young.

Peter was afraid of death.

Lazarus was dead.

John was self-righteous.

Naomi was a widow.

Paul was a persecutor of the church.

Moses was a murderer.

Jonah ran from God's will.

Miriam was a gossip.

Gideon and Thomas both doubted.

Jeremiah was depressed and suicidal.

Elijah was burned-out.

John the Baptist was a loudmouth.

Martha was a worry-wart.

Noah got drunk.

Did I mention that Moses had a short fuse?
So did Peter, Paul—well, lots of folks did.

(author unknown, "Why Would God
Want *Me*?" gatewaytojesus.com/
encouragingwritingspage1.html)

We all have some deficit, some reason that God should never choose us, but He does. God doesn't require an interview for salvation. He is not prejudiced or partial. He loves us in spite of our faults.

"Why Would God Want ME?" concludes with a conversation between Jesus and the devil.

Satan says, "You're not worthy."
Jesus says, "So what? I Am."
Satan looks back and sees our mistakes.
God looks back and sees the Cross.

God wants you, and He takes you as you are!

Don't Be Surprised by Trouble

The Bible talks about suffering so much that I wonder why we are shocked when it comes our way.

"Beloved, do not be surprised at the fiery trial when it comes upon you to test you, as though something strange were happening to you" (1 Pet. 4:12 ESV). Suffering will come and go, but we are to remain the same. If God allows us to suffer, it is so He can use our trials to make us stronger, better people. Faith is useless if it is never tested. It is easy to talk about faith, but we must walk in faith to prove we truly have it. Exercising our faith is like lifting weights. It is hard, but it increases our strength and makes our spiritual muscles larger. When we face challenges in life and use our faith, our faith grows.

Some of our suffering comes through other people. The things they do to us and the things they don't do for us can hurt. I urge you not to expect perfection from any person. If you want to be in relationships, you will have to be willing to be hurt at times because that is just what happens. Show mercy and be quick to forgive, and it will end your suffering. We are to bear with the failings of the weak (see Gal. 6:2), and we should remember that other people have to bear with our failings, too.

Perhaps we should be more concerned about the devil leaving us alone than we are about his attacking us. If he isn't bothering us, it may mean we are not bothering him. After many years of experience in ministry and with the devil, I am no longer surprised when fiery ordeals come to test my quality. I don't like them and I would rather not have them, but they don't shock me.

I realize that the devil hates it when we show love or try to help people in need, or when the gospel is preached and people are being saved. He may hate it and try to stir up trouble, but the battle is already won. We learn endurance as we go through trials and tribulations. In simple terms I think this means that we learn to outlast the devil. Just as he left Jesus in the wilderness after he had finished testing Him, say-

> *We learn to outlast the devil.*

ing he would wait for a more opportune time, so he will leave us if we stand firm on God's Word as Jesus did (see Luke 4:1–13). The devil will wait for another opportunity, but we need not fear, because the battle belongs to the Lord and we are more than conquerors through Christ Who loves us (see Rom. 8:37).

Undeserved Suffering

If anyone ever suffered and did not deserve it, it was Jesus! All of His suffering was for us. He bore injustice so we could be justified before God. If a person has done something evil, he may expect to suffer, but doing something right and then suffering for it is especially hard to bear. Peter said it is better to suffer unjustly for doing good, if that should be God's will, than it is to suffer justly for doing evil (see 1 Pet. 3:17).

We say that we want to be like Jesus, but do we really? The following Scripture passage is difficult to take in, but if we truly want to be like Jesus, we must accept what it says.

> For this is a gracious thing, when, mindful of God, one endures sorrows while suffering unjustly. For what credit is it if, when you sin and are beaten for it, you endure? But if when you do good and suffer for it you endure, this is a gracious thing in the sight of God. For to this you have been called, because Christ also suffered for you, leaving you an example, so that you might follow in his steps.
>
> 1 Peter 2:19–21 ESV

This passage says that it is good in God's sight if we endure suffering we don't deserve and that we have actually been called to do so if we intend to follow in Jesus' footsteps. Remember that my definition of *endure* means "to outlast the devil," so the next time you feel you have done good and are suffering anyway, just remind the devil that you are happy to walk the same path that Jesus walked and that you are fully convinced that God will reward you for your faithfulness.

If God is fighting our battles for us, why do we still suffer? Some battles are longer than others, and at times we will need to take the apostle Paul's advice: Having done everything the crisis demands, stand firmly in your place (see Eph. 6:13). The fact that God fights our battles for us doesn't mean we never get wounded. Our wounds will heal and we won't have scars, but we will be stronger in our faith and able to endure more the next time the enemy attacks. Each battle gives us experience with the faithfulness of God, and nothing is better than experience.

God's Word says that Jesus gained obedience through what He suffered, and that equipped Him to become the "Author and Source" of our salvation (see Heb. 5:8–9 AMPC). He was wounded for our transgressions and by His wounds we are healed and made whole (see Isa. 53:5; 1 Pet. 2:24). It may just be that in our times of unjust suffering we are also being prepared and equipped to help someone else. The job of healing wounded souls wasn't finished when Jesus left this earth to return to His place at the right hand of God; He simply turned it over to us. So let's be determined to help as many people as we can for as long as we are alive. The devil will fight against us, but God will fight for us, and we know who wins! Remember, the Word of God promises that even as we go through much difficulty, we are more than conquerors through Christ Who loves us (see Rom. 8:37). Let's always remember the promise of 1 Corinthians 15:57 (my paraphrase):

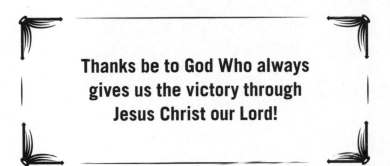

**Thanks be to God Who always
gives us the victory through
Jesus Christ our Lord!**

Do you have a real relationship with Jesus?

God loves you! He created you to be a special, unique, one-of-a-kind individual, and He has a specific purpose and plan for your life. And through a personal relationship with your Creator—God—you can discover a way of life that will truly satisfy your soul.

No matter who you are, what you've done, or where you are in your life right now, God's love and grace are greater than your sin—your mistakes. Jesus willingly gave His life so you can receive forgiveness from God and have new life in Him. He's just waiting for you to invite Him to be your Savior and Lord.

If you are ready to commit your life to Jesus and follow Him, all you have to do is ask Him to forgive your sins and give you a fresh start in the life you are meant to live. Begin by praying this prayer...

Lord Jesus, thank You for giving Your life for me and forgiving me of my sins so I can have a personal relationship with You. I am sincerely sorry for the mistakes I've made, and I know I need You to help me live right.

Your Word says in Romans 10:9, "If you declare with your mouth, 'Jesus is Lord,' and believe in your heart that God raised him from the dead, you will be saved" (NIV). I believe You are the Son of God and confess You as my Savior and Lord. Take me just as I am, and work in my heart, making me the person You want me to be. I want to live for You, Jesus, and I am so grateful that You are giving me a fresh start in my new life with You today.

I love You, Jesus!

It's so amazing to know that God loves us so much! He wants to have a deep, intimate relationship with us that grows every day as we spend time with Him in prayer and Bible study. And we want to encourage you in your new life in Christ.

Please visit joycemeyer.org/salvation to request Joyce's book *A New Way of Living*, which is our gift to you. We also have other free resources online to help you make progress in pursuing everything God has for you.

Congratulations on your fresh start in your life in Christ! We hope to hear from you soon.

ABOUT THE AUTHOR

JOYCE MEYER is one of the world's leading practical Bible teachers. A *New York Times* best-selling author, Joyce's books have helped millions of people find hope and restoration through Jesus Christ. Joyce's programs, *Enjoying Everyday Life* and *Everyday Answers with Joyce Meyer*, air around the world on television, radio, and the internet. Through Joyce Meyer Ministries, Joyce teaches internationally on a number of topics with a particular focus on how the Word of God applies to our everyday lives. Her candid communication style allows her to share openly and practically about her experiences so others can apply what she has learned to their lives.

Joyce has authored more than one hundred books, which have been translated into more than one hundred languages, and more than 65 million of her books have been distributed worldwide. Bestsellers include *Power Thoughts*; *The Confident Woman*; *Look Great, Feel Great*; *Starting Your Day Right*; *Ending Your Day Right*; *Approval Addiction*; *How to Hear from God*; *Beauty for Ashes*; and *Battlefield of the Mind*.

Joyce's passion to help hurting people is foundational to the vision of Hand of Hope, the missions arm of Joyce Meyer Ministries. Hand of Hope provides worldwide humanitarian outreaches such as feeding programs, medical care, orphanages, disaster response, human trafficking intervention and rehabilitation, and much more—always sharing the love and Gospel of Christ.

JOYCE MEYER MINISTRIES
U.S. & FOREIGN OFFICE ADDRESSES

Joyce Meyer Ministries
P.O. Box 655
Fenton, MO 63026
USA
(636) 349-0303

Joyce Meyer Ministries—Canada
P.O. Box 7700
Vancouver, BC V6B 4E2
Canada
(800) 868-1002

Joyce Meyer Ministries—Australia
Locked Bag 77
Mansfield Delivery Centre
Queensland 4122
Australia
(07) 3349 1200

Joyce Meyer Ministries—England
P.O. Box 1549
Windsor SL4 1GT
United Kingdom
01753 831102

Joyce Meyer Ministries—South Africa
P.O. Box 5
Cape Town 8000
South Africa
(27) 21-701-1056

OTHER BOOKS BY JOYCE MEYER

Love Out Loud
The Love Revolution
Making Good Habits, Breaking Bad Habits
Making Marriage Work (previously published as *Help Me—I'm Married!*)
Me and My Big Mouth! *
The Mind Connection *
Never Give Up!
Never Lose Heart
New Day, New You
Overload
The Penny
Perfect Love (previously published as *God Is Not Mad at You*) *
The Power of Being Positive
The Power of Being Thankful
The Power of Determination
The Power of Forgiveness
The Power of Simple Prayer
Power Thoughts
Power Thoughts Devotional
Reduce Me to Love
The Secret Power of Speaking God's Word
The Secrets of Spiritual Power
The Secret to True Happiness
Seven Things That Steal Your Joy
Start Your New Life Today
Starting Your Day Right
Straight Talk
Teenagers Are People Too!
Trusting God Day by Day
The Word, the Name, the Blood
Woman to Woman
You Can Begin Again

JOYCE MEYER SPANISH TITLES

Belleza en Lugar de Cenizas (*Beauty for Ashes*)
Buena Salud, Buena Vida (*Good Health, Good Life*)
Cambia Tus Palabras, Cambia Tu Vida (*Change Your Words, Change Your Life*)
El Campo de Batalla de la Mente (*Battlefield of the Mind*)
Como Formar Buenos Habitos y Romper Malos Habitos (*Making Good Habits, Breaking Bad Habits*)

La Conexión de la Mente (The Mind Connection)
Dios No Está Enojado Contigo (God Is Not Mad at You)
La Dosis de Aprobación (The Approval Fix)
Efesios: Comentario Biblico (Ephesians: Biblical Commentary)
Empezando Tu Día Bien (Starting Your Day Right)
Hazte Un Favor a Ti Mismo...Perdona (Do Yourself a Favor...Forgive)
Madre Segura de sí Misma (The Confident Mom)
Pensamientos de Poder (Power Thoughts)
Sanidad Para el Alma de Una Mujer (Healing the Soul of a Woman)
Santiago: Comentario Bíblico (James: Biblical Commentary)
Sobrecarga (Overload) *
Termina Bien tu Día (Ending Your Day Right)
Usted Puede Comenzar de Nuevo (You Can Begin Again)
Viva Valientemente (Living Courageously)

* Study Guide available for this title

BOOKS BY DAVE MEYER

Life Lines